Thomas Broughton

The political History of John Bull

Or, The true Engl shman, neither a Republican nor an Aristocrat

Thomas Broughton

The political History of John Bull
Or, The true Englishman, neither a Republican nor an Aristocrat

ISBN/EAN: 9783337077617

Printed in Europe, USA, Canada, Australia, Japan

Cover: Foto ©ninafisch / pixelio.de

More available books at **www.hansebooks.com**

THE POLITICAL HISTORY

OF

JOHN BULL;

OR,

THE TRUE ENGLISHMAN,

NEITHER A REPUBLICAN NOR AN ARISTOCRAT.

—————I knew their political juggling,
Things which ftartle Reafon, and make me deem
Not this, nor that, but every Conftitution falfe.

ADDRESSED BY JOHN BULL

TO THE

RIGHT HONOURABLE WILLIAM PITT.

ALSO,

REMARKS

ON THE PRESENT STATE OF THE ELECTIVE

POWER OF THE PEOPLE,

AND

THE CONSTITUTION OF PARLIAMENT,

WITH PROPOSITIONS FOR ACCOMPLISHING AN EQUAL AND ADE-
QUATE REPRESENTATION OF

THE COMMONS OF GREAT-BRITAIN

IN PARLIAMENT,

AND

A CONSTITUTIONAL MODE OF REFORM.

———————

BY THOMAS BROUGHTON.

———————

Read not to contradict and confute, nor to believe and take for granted, nor to
find Talk and Difcourfe, but to weigh and confider.   BACON.

———————

LONDON:

PRINTED FOR AND SOLD BY J. OWEN, NO. 168, PICCADILLY,
AND J. BEW IN PATERNOSTER-ROW.

6

1792.

ADVERTISEMENT.

AS the obfervations contained in the following Papers were made prior to the
recent debate in the Houfe of Commons on
the neceffity of a Parliamentary Reform, and
before a number of independent Gentlemen
affociated to effect that grand purpofe, it is but
a juft tribute to the patriotifm and refpectabi-
lity of thofe real friends of the people to obferve, that they anfwer the defcription, both
in principles and worth, of thofe truly independent characters, who are here reprefented
as the only proper perfons to effect this effential meafure. And as they wifely proceed on
conftitutional grounds, they merit the unanimous fupport of the whole nation; that
thefe are my humble, unbiaffed fentiments,
will, I truft, be proved from the freedom of
the following cafual remarks; in which it will
appear that JOHN BULL is neither a Minifte-
rialift nor Anti-minifterialift, nor Whig nor

Tory.

Tory. He cannot reconcile the idea of a division of the common interest: he is convinced the very name of Party augurs a hostile intention against his liberties; and after much conversation we had together on this subject, it was with infinite concern on his part he concluded, that he could not look up with confidence to either side for the support of his real interest: he was afraid that those who avowedly opposed Ministers in every measure were in pursuit of the Hesperian Garden; and if they could slay the dragon, they would take possession of the golden fruit, and notwithstanding all their fair promises, still leave him in the lurch. He had no hopes left; secret and corrupt influence had thrown a contempt on patriotism, and established a paradoxical system, wherein integrity and abilities were considered as hostile, and cunning and treachery alone found favour; and he had now no other alternative than to encourage the union of independent country gentlemen and citizens to obtain a

free

free and equal reprefentation, that practical
Government might combine with the admirable theory of his Conftitution. He was a
plain Englifhman, unhacknied in the arts of
managing a Parliament or a Party ; but inflexibly determined to maintain the free operation of his Conftitution with his life and fortune. This he wifhed might be underftood
to be a principle he drew in with his breath ;
it lived with him, and could only be annihi-
hilated with his perfon. As for myfelf, who
am but the humble vehicle of his fentiments,
I beg leave to obferve, if in the generous ardor
of liberty, and the fincere reverence for a Conftitution eftablifhed by the wifdom of fuccef-
five ages, fome propofitions and terms fhould
efcape me of too pofitive a nature, every true
friend to conftitutional liberty will put a liberal conftruction on every attempt to defend
thofe principles, which, for this laft century,
have attracted the admiration, as well as excited the envy of all Europe ; and every fuch
friend to our Conftitution will overlook the

animated

animated manner a free difcuffion of its abufes
demands, as an unavoidable effect of the true
fpirit of liberty. It is therefore with deference
and refpect I appeal to the underftanding of
every reader, that if my expreffions on the
abufe in the National Reprefentation, which
is the leading fubject of inveftigation, fhould
appear to be conveyed with too much fervor,
I hope to find an apology in their own feelings. At the fame time I am confcious, that
neither fatire can influence the candid and
impartial, nor warmth of expreffion convince
the better informed. My object will be accomplifhed, if my endeavours fhall induce
one from the many better qualified to refume
a fubject the moft important to every Briton.

THOMAS BROUGHTON.

Auguft 8*th,* 1792.

TO

THE RIGHT HONOURABLE

WILLIAM PITT.

SIR,

THE language of flattery is grateful to the ear; and though it conveys an in-sult to the sense, the understanding applauds the sacrifice, and deals to it both favour and friendship. But the voice of sincerity frequently conveys a sting which wounds the pride of self-love; and notwithstanding the displeasure it excites, is palliated by the inward conviction of its truth; a real friend is too often considered in the light of an enemy. These prefatory remarks disclose to you my intention; which, as a man loyal to his King, and zealous in the support of the civil and religious liberties confirmed at the Revolution, duty rather imposes than choice dictates, the detailing of vices which are growing on the Constitution.

I lament

I lament that you, Sir, formed by nature and education for eminence, adorned with the beft private virtues, and graced with abilities early matured by your immortal father, fhould become a facrifice to *Borough traffic*. But I more than lament, that a Conftitution in its component parts fo well conftructed, in its effect fo aptly defigned for public profperity and private happinefs, fhould in its Democratic part, by that traffic, labour under an Ariftocratic gangrene.

In your integrity your friends may place a confidence; but individual rectitude, cannot ftem the contagion of former Adminiftrations. Abufes are too frefh in the public mind to induce it to repofe implicitly in a fallible man. The wifdom of paft ages has given to pofterity the independence of Parliament as the facred palladium of Britifh liberty. But this bulwark of freedom is held by fo precarious a tenure, that for many years paft the abfolute neceffity of a Reform in the National

Repre-

Reprefentation has refounded from every
quarter of the kingdom. The rights of the
people demand an equal and free reprefentation. On this point the collected wifdom of
the nation centers. The great majority of
people are impreffed with one fentiment,
" That the Conftitution is a glorious fabric."
But the chief pillar of its fupport has been for
years decaying; the ftamina is contaminated;
the freedom of election is perverted, and by
that perverfion the Conftitution of Parliament
is violated. It is this corrupted part of the
Conftitution that affords to republicanifm a
triumph. It is this which gives to faction
a form and figure.

Painful as the conviction of thefe facts are
in the breaft of every true Englifhman, yet
the facred maxim of his Conftitution, which
gives a remedy when a right is invaded, ex-
alts his mind to its true dignity, that with an
equanimity which equality and juftice only
produces, he can look up to power with a refolution

folution which will triumph over oppreffion, and maintain his rights. No one act, therefore, can you atchieve that will enhance your name fo much with pofterity, as to meet the times with a temperate reform. This is the great crifis of your public career; your patriotifm and your reputation are at iffue; embrace the tide now flowing to immortal honour; the wifhes, the endeavours, and the interefts of the fober, independent part of the nation are with you; face the enemy in the firft inftance, and the levelling hydra will fink into oblivion; it gains ftrength from your fears; it merely exifts by the delay of a meafure which will *conciliate all difaffection,* preferve the texture and genius of our happy conftitution, and redound to the honour of the firft free kingdom in the world.

Thefe, Sir, are the fentiments of a loyal people; men impreffed with the love of their country; men whofe ardent wifhes are to draw from the wholefome ftatutes of the land

their

their priftine vigour, whofe efforts will be to maintain the energy of their reprefentation.

In reply to this it will be alledged, and I am ready to meet the hacknied affertions, that it is much eafier to complain than to remedy; that materials are eafily found, but defects are not fo readily fupplied. Innovations are hurtful, operating on particulars, they excite prejudice. Let us not touch the bafis, left the breath of anarchy fhould diffipate the fabric. Such ignoble fentiments on a conftitutional neceffary meafure, if not interefted, are unworthy of an enlightened people, and degrade a free nation ; all ranks of people reverence royalty; every true Englifhman will fupport the Crown ; but there is not a man but knows the Crown has no longer any analogy to liberty than as the reprefentatives of the people are independent, and the Parliament free.

If my refpect furmounted my duty, I might have forborn to have reminded you of your

illuftrious

illuſtrious father. May the filial remembrance of him ſtimulate you to this glorious purſuit. The eſtabliſhing of conſtitutional liberty on its true foundation is worthy of honour; it will acquire you immortal fame. Permit me to ſay, it is your duty to ſet at defiance the Ariſtocratic party in the Houſe of Commons. Your firſt engagement was to promote and effect a reform in Parliament.

The olive branch now courts the laurel; remove therefore the maſk from the Genius of the Conſtitution, and the nation will entwine your brow with the emblems of liberty. Recorded honours will hover round your name. The diſappointed levellers may cavil at your ſucceſs; but future ages will engrave your virtues on marble. Animated with a true zeal for the real intereſts of the kingdom,

I am,

Right Honourable SIR,

Your Friend,

JOHN BULL.

CONTENTS.

SECTION I.

SECTION II.

SECTION III.

SECTION IV.

SECTION V.

SECTION

THE

POLITICAL HISTORY

OF

JOHN BULL.

SECTION I.

A brief Sketch of the Character of JOHN BULL, *with a prefatory Dialogue, containing Remarks on the Republican and Aristocratic Doctrines of the Day.*

AS a man cannot in all cafes fpeak of him-felf without the imputation of vanity, it may be neceffary firft to premife the character of JOHN BULL. A favourable prepoffeffion, which engages the heart, and attaches the mind, is a favourable circumftance, which, though not al-ways within our reach, merits our utmoft ende-vours to attain. If this attempt fhould fail, it muft be attributed to a deficiency of talents in the au-thor juftly to delineate his worthy appellant. For if generous principles difplay the dignity of man, John Bull by Nature poffeffes the beft gifts of Heaven; philanthropy ennobles his heart, and in-fpires his mind with the moft liberal fentiments;

B   in

in which courage and charity contending for eminence, honour interfered, and united them. Dignified as he is in difpofition, yet he is too credu-
lous, which arifes from thofe principles of fecurity
he had early imbibed from his excellent Conftitution; and all his views and defigns are marked
with that open franknefs, that manly affurance and
dignity of conduct, which fo particularly diftin-
guifh him from the natives of arbitrary States. A
combination of fuch noble qualities naturally produces a temper which is fuperior to faction; with
contemptuous difdain he looks on, while Envy is
biting her lips, and Ambition is treading the air.
But when Injuftice unites her iron hand, and
tramples on his rights, he exerts himfelf with that
energy and effect which have ever diftinguifhed
his patriotic meafures, and will always preferve his
freedom. Such being the general traits of his
character, it cannot be expected his plain language will accord with the fophiftry of interefted politicians. On the contrary, perceiving a
regular progreffion of immorality, which threatens
his Conftitution, keeping pace with fafhion, folly,
and luxury, John Bull will have his rights afferted
in a true Englifh ftyle; in which if a dafh of ec-
centricity fo congenial with his nature fhould appear, his found principles and good intentions
muft apologize. Agreeable to his engagement, he
now vifited me; and after the ufual congratulations,
we entered on bufinefs.

John

John Bull. If you are, Sir, a plain lettered man, and free from the bias of party, I fhall not be dif-appointed having engaged you to affert my rights.

The Author. Really, Sir, I had no reafon to ex-pect that honour from a man of your importance, having no claim on the world for poffeffing that . humble talent; neither fhould I venture to affume fuch a claim, but on fo plain fubject as your rights. By trade I know you to be a dealer in facts; I fhall be proud, therefore, to tranfcribe your ledger, and draw out your bills on your debtors. To party I am unknown, and by the Conftitution, free; un-der your protection, I may then venture with con-fidence; at leaft my beft endeavours will be to defend the Conftitution, and merit your approbation.

John Bull. The privilege of fpeaking truth being denied, her facred value is loft; and the tongue tortured by reftraint, or intereft, feeks the colours of fophiftry to fhade the dictates of the heart. Hence the variety of opinions on the fimple theme of liberty keeps pace with the growth of politicians, to which the French Revolution has afforded a fruitful feafon. For here I find a Republican level-ling his predatory principles againft me; and there an Ariftocrat endeavouring to ftrangle me. And for this long time paft, I have been put in fear of my life; and without a transfufion of new blood into my veins, I fhall not be able to withftand

their

their attacks; for I find my Conftitution much impaired by infractions made on it in my youth; and my infirmities have much increafed fince the paralytic ftroke, which deprived me of my voice in St. Stephen's Chapel, where for many years paft I have fat as an inanimate idol in the Oracle of Delphi, to fanction the previous refolutions of the Priefts of a Council. But perceiving there are now two partries, both enemies to the health of my Conftitution, the one pulling the cords or ftamina of my exiftence at one end, and the other pulling at the other, I am determined to make good my hold, to prevent their breaking; for my anceftors left me this facred axiom—" That we fhould all pull toge- " ther, and form three feparate pillars for the fupport " of ONE GRAND FABRIC," which I am bound fa- credly to maintain. But the regaining of my pub- lic voice being abfolutely neceffary to affure my right to collateral aid and equal benefit, I fhall depute you to affert my privileges, and refpectfully fuggeft to the Higher Powers a mode of Reform in my Reprefentation. Be candid and impartial; we have but one intereft; we can have but one wifh. It is the birth-right of Englifhmen to keep the Britifh Oak of Liberty free from corrofions. Let it be our pride, as it is our duty, that pofterity may find it flourifhing in the greateft fplendour.

The Author. Indeed, Sir, you utter your com- plaints with fo much emphafis, I find you have
already

already made fome advance on my feelings. I fhall beg to propofe, that we make our joint remarks on popular topics in this Section; during the courfe of which I fhall have an opportunity of catching your ftyle; and alfo that your complaints, your interefts, and your rights, may make fuch an impreffion on me, that when I write the dictates of your heart, I may find them equally accord with the fentiments of my own mind. This is actually neceffary before I can make remarks on your political hiftory.

John Bull. What flows from the dictates of the heart men in general admire, which can only be attributed to fympathy; for, on fixed principles, you will find theory and practice at continual variance. But the heart, though involved in every intricate evolution of the mind, ftill retains the human bias.

The Author. Philofophy and liberty, it is faid, are infeparable; and certainly it would reflect a cenfurable ftupidity in me not to admire and congratulate you on their progrefs. And fhall it now be faid the prefent age muft ftill wear the garment of Liberty with that tattered appendage of Norman rigour, the Borough Reprefentation, becaufe we have not a Juftinian to refcind it? Let the ignoble thought be banifhed, and the Britifh Conftitution be purified.

John

John Bull. A great political character fays, we cherifh our prejudices becaufe they are prejudices. Under this idea, I imagine, he termed the people a fwinifh multitude. This pillar of hereditary rights and arbitrary claims will eventually find a free State the wrong market for his principles; it being my will to roufe from patriotic apathy, and examine if indolence and fupinenefs have not occafioned a breach in the bulwark of our freedom; and probably in the fting of difaffection may be found a truth, which being embraced may preferve the fpirit of the Conftitution.

The Author. However we may differ from the principles of difaffected writers, we are not to difregard fome truths which they convey. But it is become a fafhion among men to defpife truth, becaufe it affects their pride; and a man is equally a depredator, whether he attacks another's purfe or his pride; fo the law conftrues truth, which Nature ordained the fountain of virtue; but now it is become the libellous pander of Juftice.

John Bull. Let the lawyers torture words, and diffect Acts of Parliament, keep to the letter of my conftitutional right, and deal freely with the Republican and Ariftocratic doctrines of the day; and if it fhould appear to have a tendency rather to amufe the mind than to convince the judgment, let it be remembered, if fatire be ever in the leaft allowable,

allowable, it is when it has for its object Vice, and for its end Truth.

The Author. A man may certainly venture to hold up the mirror of Truth under your patronage, particularly when the chief object is his country's benefit; and if from the refult of our inveftiga- tion abufes fhould appear, it becomes the duty of Government to apply immediate and effectual re- medies.

John Bull. Abufes exift which require neither fcience nor ingenuity to explore.

The Author. And from thofe abufes have arifen our enormous national debt, which hangs a dead weight from the neck of Britannia. Yet her fons make a figure, as if fhe were mounted in a golden car. Thefe are glittering days!

John Bull. Public credit keeps them floating on the tide, where, if they would attend to my voice, they fhould continue to be wafted, but not till an ebb takes place will they liften to me.

The Author. And by a new philofophy *, this enormous debt is declared to be a great national

---

* See the Effays of the Marquis de Cafaux and George Crawford, which proceed upon the idea that it is abfurd and injurious to attempt to diminifh the national debt.

B 4   bleffing;

bleffing; for as neceffity is the parent of invention, fpeculation has now arrived to the very fummit of perfection. The tax-gatherers give a fpur to induftry; they quicken the genius, and mature the invention of a whole family; they give energy to trade, life to commerce, and fpirit to the whole nation. One novelty fucceeds another, till curiofity is loft in a maze. Medical men, for inftance, have added fome hundred drugs to the *Materia Medica*, hitherto unknown, whofe virtues are grand fpecifics. Indeed, the knowledge of Galen and Hippocrates is wholly exploded by the deep refearches of modern advertifing empirics of health —Paint, Patch, and Perfume.

John Bull. I will venture to impart a fecret to you. Thefe grand fpecifics poffefs two virtues; the firft enables them to fet up a chariot and make a figure, and the fecond enables them to pay the taxes which fupport the national debt.

The Author. Which fully prove Neceffity to be the parent of Invention. The tax-gatherers, again, have in an amazing degree fharpened the wits of the lawyers, who are now become fupremely fpeculative. They can foon convince a man that a light pair of heels is better than a fafe confcience. For if he brings in a *fat* caufe into court, notwithftanding he may have reafon and truth on his fide, yet they immediately throw it into the fcale of felf-
interest;

intereft; and to incline the balance in their favour, they torture, flice, and trim the letter of the law, till he is fixed with enormous cofts, and then he muft either run or pay.

John Bull. Taxes muft be paid; the national debt muft be fupported.

The Author. The tax-gatherers have alfo thrown a new light on trade. Firft, the bankers, to fupport needy tradefmen, oppreffed with taxes, and the confequent advance of the articles of life, difcount the manufactured paper of thofe who are of fair fame. Secondly, the wholefale traders encourage young men to fet up retailers, without capitals, who have the repute of having been fober and fteady affiftants to eminent traders. Thefe are neceffary connexions to fupport fictitious paper, and create large returns. Hence the numerous *accomodations*, from the loweft mechanic to the higheft merchant; hence the increafe of country banks; hence the increafe of attornies; hence the increafe of brokers; and, finally, hence the increafe of bankrupts.

John Bull. Taxes muft be paid; the national debt muft be fupported.

The Author. The tax-gatherers rout out the lower clafs of people from their peaceful habitations, and

the

the advance of common neceffaries induce them to forfake honeft avocations. Hence the increafe of fwindlers, mail-robbers, highwaymen, pickpockets, &c. hence the aggrandizement of the colony of Botany Bay to our antient kingdom, and the rapid increafe of its population.

John Bull. Taxes muft be paid; the national debt muft be fupported.

The Author. Your replies being fo uniform, you are certainly of opinion the morality of the people is the leaft confideration, when the public good is to be confulted. I may reckon you a difciple of Mandeville, who affirms, that private vices are public benefits. The taxes muft be paid un-doubtedly; but by what means can public credit be fecured?

John Bull. By the brokers keeping up the price of ftocks *, notwithftanding it gives the advantage to foreigners to buy and fell to our wrong.

---

* The fpirit of ftock-jobbing is to the fpirit of trade what the fpirit of faction is to the fpirit of liberty. The tendency of both is to advance the intereft of a few worthlefs individuals, at the expence of the whole community. The confequence of both, if ever they prevail to the ruin of trade and liberty, muft be, that the harpies will ftarve in imaginary wealth, and that the children of faction, like the iron race of Cadmus, will de-ftroy one another.

Bolingbroke's Remarks, Hift. Eng. p. 169.

But

But this was an unneceffary remark ; for if we are reduced to the laft guinea, we have an ample fupply of Bank and other paper.

The Author. A fortunate refource to fupport public credit.

John Bull. As the national debt increafed, public credit advanced. It may therefore be very dangerous to remain long at peace ; for the increafe of commerce and wealth might reduce the national debt, and confequently lower our credit.

The Author. The national debt then is a great bleffing; it is the bafis of public credit, and muft not be reduced.

John Bull. Again, another weighty confideration. Why, it may be very dangerous to remain long at peace. Inglorious wars and armaments have happily created a number of public offices, and provided for a hoft of excifemen, commiffaries, contractors, agents, &c. befides placemen and penfioners, and a ftanding army. If the increafe of commerce and wealth is not checked by a war, the national debt will be reduced, and we may unfortunately have all thefe men thrown on the public, and our credit lowered.

The

The Author. That would be a great national evil, indeed.

John Bull. We have dared Spain; we have ſtrained at Ruſſia; and for the maintenance and promotion of the officers of the Crown, the army and navy, and the ſupport of public credit, it does not appear that we can fairly exiſt another twelve-month without an actual war.

The Author. Reduction is a more formidable word than war; it conveys a greater trepidation than to be drafted on a hazardous ſiege. A long peace will bring us into this dilemma. The national debt is a great bleſſing; it is the baſis of public credit, and muſt not be reduced.

John Bull. Very fortunately, the preſent war in India keeps up the ſpirit of the nation, affords to ſpeculation her vital matter, and ſupports the new philoſophy you ſpeak of, which declares, that as our burthens increaſe, and the national debt is augmented, we grow in wealth and proſperity, and enjoy every bleſſing.

The Author. A moſt fortunate circumſtance to ſupport public credit.

John Bull. After an indulgence of other people's opinions, I may be permitted to give my own private one.

The Author. That will afford me pleasure, as I am sure it will be ingenuous.

John Bull. First, I consider public credit naturally draws with it and promotes private credit. As the nation, therefore, has gone to extraordinary lengths, by mortgaging to support inglorious and expensive wars, the age has become gay, showy, false, and flattering. Fictitious and other paper money creates a deceptive appearance, and gives a false colour to property, which promotes luxury, and luxury increases the growth of effeminacy and vice, which induce men to treat religion as a chimera; and this is the first step to corrupt the morals, and ruin the State.

Secondly, Public credit being wholly dependant, and combined with the executive power, and every year becoming aggrandized *, we are, by luxury, immorality, and neglect of patriotism, gra-

* The instruments of power are not perhaps so open and avowed as they formerly were, and therefore are the less liable to jealous and invidious reflections, but they are not the weaker upon that account. In short, our national debt and taxes, besides the inconveniences before mentioned, have also in their natural consequences thrown such a weight of power into the executive scale of Government, as we cannot think was intended by our patriot ancestors, who gloriously struggled for the abolition of the then formidable parts of the prerogative, and by an unaccountable want of foresight, established this system in their stead.   *Blackst. Comment. vol. I. p.* 387.

dually

dually sliding into that arbitrary state from which
France has recently wrested herself. She once before was free, and enjoyed her three independent
Estates. But from the baneful practice of corruptly
influencing the representatives of the people, they
became, by the aggrandizement of the Crown, con-
solidated into an absolute power *.

The Author. Your arguments fully convince me
of the necessity of reclaiming your elective power.
The national debt having created so many new offices and new places of every description, which,
being entirely at the pleasure of the Crown, has given to the Executive Power a proportion of weight
so far superior to the other constituent parts, that
it may fairly be said to hold the scales of the Constitution in its hand; or, in other words, the
legislative body at its devotion, of which collusion
Montesquieu foretells the loss of our freedom.
" As all human things," he observes, " must

---

* *Mem.* Philip de Comines—Duplex Mezray—By exerting
all his powers and address in influencing the elections of representatives, by bribing and over-awing the members, and by various changes which he artfully made in the form of her delibe-
rations. Lewis the Eleventh acquired such entire direction of
the national assemblies, that from being the vigilant guardians
of the privileges and property of the people, he rendered them
tamely subservient in protecting the odious measures of his reign.
Phil. de Comines, vol. I. He first taught other modern Princes
the fatal art of becoming arbitrary, by corrupting the fountain
of public liberty.

" have

" have an end, the State we are fpeaking of will
" lofe its liberty. It will perifh when the legifla-
" tive power fhall become more corrupt than the
" executive *."

John Bull. It is too evident the national debt,
by thus ftrengthening the Crown, has deftroyed
that equilibrium, which, by the Conftitution is
placed in the reprefentatives of the people, by influencing a majority, independent of the elective
power of their conftituents. If I wanted a proof
to fubftantiate this fact, I need but recur to the
late Ruffian armament. When it was notorious
that this equilibrium was loft, the general fentiment was made known through the medium of
the prefs. It was this cenforian privilege which
wrefted liberty from the hands of power. It is this
palladium of our rights which explores the fecrets
of the Cabinet, and keeps magiftrates and minifters
within the line of duty, which penetrates the vi-
brations of the heart, and holds up to publie view
its evolutions.

The Author. Indeed, John Bull, you grow on
me. Every fentence convinces me of the neceffity
of a Parliamentary Reform.

John Bull. When I fpeak of a ftanding majority,
it may be neceffary to difcriminate between thofe

* Montefquieu.

acts which may be termed partial and personal, such as the Slave Trade and the Impeachment, and those public measures which gall the nation, and involve the whole body of people, such as armaments and wars. In these I have no voice. Dragged to battle like a slave against my will, and in return have my property taxed to maintain the dignity of the nation, or, in other words, the pampered pride of Treasurers, Paymasters, Agents, Commissaries, Commissioners, Contractors, Placemen and Pensioners, and other necessary evils, in a right cause, although right or wrong they uniformly support the Executive Power, and their yearly increase becomes a subject of just apprehension to the people. If there be any public virtue to be found in the nation, or a real and sincere regard for the permanency of an excellent Constitution, free elections and frequent new Parliaments will be obtained, to counteract that system of immoral policy, which was brought to maturity by a Minister *, who styled himself, *No Saint, No Spartan, No Reformer*, who treated public virtue as a bubble, and love of the country as a farce; and whose system of packed majorities, so pernicious to the liberties of the people, was practised throughout the American war. The venal and flagitious collusions of men in office under Government at various times, shew how notoriously I have been

* Sir Robert Walpole.

duped.

duped. One packed majority to grant millions
drawn from my pockets, and another packed majority to drown my voice when I demand an ex-
planation how thofe millions have been applied,
millions to this day remaining unaccounted for to
the public *. Redrefs and Reform were the two
grand objects which poffeffed Mr. Pitt's mind
when he entered into office; two fubjects worthy
of his fuperior merits. He made fome advances
which reflect a degree of honour, but having been
long filent in thefe meritorious purfuits, I am
induced to draw conclufions that eclipfe thofe abilities which fo confpicuoufly fhone forth for patriotic fplendour. His integrity to the public is
bound by his early promifes to effect a Parliamentary Reform. May his public virtues become as
confpicuous as his private, by reiterating his endeavours for this effential meafure.

The Author. If the obftacles to a Reform are remote from him, it is a duty he owes to the people
and to himfelf to undeceive their confidence—He
will be left to no choice between his duty and reputation, for it is no new axiom in politics, That
a people may be abridged of their Liberties, and
the conftituent parts of Government be violated,
confiftently with the extenfion of commerce and

* See the petition of the Freeholders of Middlefex, 1769—
repeated in an Addrefs to his Majefty by Mr. Pitt, 1783.

C   the

the increafe of wealth. The ancient Grecian and Roman States prove, that, in all free Governments as luxury increafes the fpirit of liberty decreafes. The truths afferted in your laft arguments are irrefiftible ; and I muft confefs I now feel myfelf properly influenced to affert your right to a free reprefentation. But, firft, it may be ufeful to make fome remarks on the contending enemies of the Conftitution, whofe erroneous principles cannot be rendered too general, as the more univerfally they are known, it acquires the greater fecurity. The republican champion has indulged an intemperate and mifplaced ridicule, by attacking kings in their leaft defenfible part, as individuals and men divefted of magiftracy, and by delineating a fpecious form of Government, and infinuating its purity, in order to conceal the republican poifon which he in vain endeavours to inftill into the minds of the people.

John Bull. Let us take care how we are carried away with founds. The republican doctrine is an inflammatory theme, which militates againft our Conftitution. Its purpofes are too evident; it is to fet afide our Supreme Magiftrate, in whofe perfect fafety the very exiftence of our Conftitution depends. And further, it is for levelling all diftinctions in fociety, and deftroying all thofe barriers which preferve peace and order in a ftate.

The

The Author. When he declaims againſt monarchy, he artfully makes no diſtinction between a tyrannical Government, wherein the Monarch's will is the ſupreme law, and a limited Monarchy ſuch as ours, wherein the ſupremacy is lodged in the legiſlative authority created by the community. His arguments in no inſtance apply to our monarchical form of Government, it being a maxim of the Conſtitution, *That the King can do no wrong.*

> ————————" He is ours
> " T' adminiſter, to guard, to adorn the State,
> " But not to warp or change it."

For by the Conſtitution he has appointed a Privy Council, which has the guidance of the executive power; and Miniſters of the Crown are amenable to the repreſentatives of the people, who can impeach and puniſh evil counſellors. Hence the equilibrium of the Conſtitution is ſo happily poized, that the will of the One Supreme muſt coaleſce with the wills of the many who obey.

John Bull. If there be ſuch a mutual check of one conſtituent part on the other, why is unlimited confidence ſo much debated for ? It appears to cover a myſtery which I conjecture to be an impoſition on our Conſtitution.

The Author. Unlimited confidence as naturally ariſes from the abuſe of your repreſentation, as honour among men who live by depredation.

The

The pride of office bravely dares the conftitutional few, confcious that the venal tribe have depofited their integrity for their places and their views of patronage. This or that Minifter is no more cenfurable on the general eftablifhed practice than the Grand Viziers. It is the perverfion of your elective power grown upon your excellent Conftitution fince the Revolution, and which requires only refolution and integrity in the national body to remedy.

John Bull. The truth of which is too palpable; neverthelefs, to define the limits of confidence is a matter of no fmall difficulty.

The Author. They are truly afcertained in the complex ftructure of your conftitution, whofe powers acting reciprocally one upon the other, produce a political machine, the moft beautiful and correct that ever was devifed by the wifdom of man. The theory of it has for its bafis the laws of God and Nature, general liberty, and univerfal juftice. The independent oppofition of its conftituent parts, judicioufly applying to each other for its free adminiftration to the people, is its vital principle; and this proves it to be a monument of human perfection, participating of the immutable laws of matter, which act by oppofition to produce a certain good. A thunder ftorm may menace deftruction like the American war; yet Aurora

from

from the Eaſt once more uſhers in the gladdened day, and all Nature again rejoices.

John Bull. Thus we have revived, which ſhews there is a ſolid principle in the machine which works its own deliverance.

The Author. In the theory of the Conſtitution that principle is to be found ; but in the inſtance alluded to, the theory of the Conſtitution was wholly loſt ſight of by the abuſe in your repreſentation ; and we owe much of our deliverance to a fortunate and ſingularly happy, becauſe it will ever be found a permanent circumſtance—the inſular and local ſituation of this kingdom. But to return to our ſtrictures on this republican. His principles applied to this country are an exception to common ſenſe. The people of England will ever look back to the commonwealth of the laſt century ; and reflecting on the anarchy and deſtruction of civil liberty at that period, will finally reject principles which tend to the ſame iſſue, principles which, renouncing ſubordination, create diſſenſions ; and as they ſow jealouſies, they nurſe vicious ambition, an intemperate ſpirit of dominion ſucceeds, power demurs againſt equity, and the once liberal Coſmopolite, the free Republican, becomes the haughty, arbitrary Ariſtocrat.

John

John Bull. By his laſt publication, he ſeems to
poſſeſs all the novelty of a prophet, without a miſ-
ſion; the theory of his heart is vanity, the practice
of it preſumption. Mark his own words. "I
"have not only contributed to raiſe a New Empire
"in the world, founded on a new ſyſtem of Go-
"vernment; but I have arrived at an eminence in
"political literature, the moſt difficult of all lines
"to ſucceed and excel in."—"I neither read
"books, nor ſtudied other people's opinions."—
"I thought for myſelf. Independence is my hap-
"pineſs; and I view things as they are, without
"regard to place or perſon."—"My country is
"the world; my religion to do good."—"Speak-
"ing for myſelf, my parents were not able to give
"me a ſhilling, except towards my education, yet
"I poſſeſs more of what is called conſequence in
"the world, than any one in Mr. Burke's cata-
"logue of Ariſtocrats *."

The Author. The man who vainly puffs himſelf
off, I am convinced is the laſt to obtain your confidence. Though he may be actuated by a
laudable motive, the liberty of mankind, yet his
principles are ſo predatory, his ſpeculations ſo
vague, that moderate men, who compoſe the ſober
and ſolid part of the nation, are ſhocked, and men
who exiſt by the means of Government laugh in

* Egotiſms in the Second Part of The Rights of Man.

their

their fleeve to find him but the mere offspring of faction, darting a poifon which waftes itfelf in the air before it reaches them.

John Bull. I have read, and formed a judgment not very eafily to be fhaken : I am in confequence fully convinced there is no nation in the world whofe laws breathe more of the true fpirit of freedom, and whofe various civil inftitutions are more effectually calculated to promote the happinefs and profperity of mankind than thofe of Old England ; but that they have been perverted by the abufe in my reprefentation, is a fact too notorious to be denied.

The Author. Your obfervation is very juft. The conftituent parts of our Conftitution, and the fpirit of our laws, have received the encomiums of the greateft ftatefmen and writers of moft nations. His wanton abufe of thofe inftitutions and laws has foiled him with his own weapons, by attacking principles which are good, and not confining himfelf to the practice which has been bad.

John Bull. Yet he has the prefumption to fay, Mr. Burke would refute him if he could.

The Author. I fhould entertain a mean opinion of Mr. Burke, if he defcended to refute principles which in this country confute themfelves. What

man

man of fortune but would riſk his life, rather than
be robbed of half his annual income by a metaphy-
ſical mob.   Such an equalizing of property is not
in the nature of things.   There will always be a
Lazarus as well as a Dives.   His levelling principles may proſper a century hence in Botany Bay,
as they were the beſt calculated for America.   The
Americans had no Princes to cut up, no Nobility
to trim, nor any Biſhops to feaſt on ; they were all
in a ſtate of equality.   Under ſuch circumſtances,
a republic ſeems to promiſe to every man the
higheſt enjoyment of liberty.   But experience
proves, that men deviate from firſt principles. The
mind of man is reſtleſs and aſpiring.   The aggrandizement of wealth breaks the bond of equality,
and creates power; power creates influence, and
influence generates corruption.   Hence all the republics in the civilized world, Holland, Venice,
Berne, &c. &c. being founded on a levelling ſyſtem, have degenerated into ſlaviſh ariſtocracies,
which are compleat and poſitive refutations of his
republican principles.   Different gradations of
rank, from the peaſant to the Prince, and ſubordination among mankind, are founded in Nature,
confirmed by Scripture hiſtory ; and no new-
fangled repreſentative levelling ſyſtem can alter
that which forms a part of the Conſtitution of the
world.   It may derange, like a ſtorm, the order
of things for a time, but principles will ever return
to the channel Nature has decreed them to courſe
in.

in. America is in her infancy, and the boasted perfection * of her polity already at variance with its principle; and France, to the infinite mortification of this flaming Republican, has widely differed from his pure representative system, by establishing an hereditary Monarchy. She found without that key-stone to bind the whole, her Government would be enfeebled, and her Constitution, doubtful as it may be, would be rendered more precarious. His comparative statements of the expences of Government in England and America, is of all his attempts the most futile. If the income allowed to the Supreme Chief in America amounts to no more than the income of the Mayor of one of our cities, is it not idle to suppose his Majesty should be reduced to near the same establishment? It is the honest pride of the citizens of London to support their municipal establishment in its present dignity; and it is the noble emulation of Britons, and their peculiar boast, that the energy of their Executive Power can command other nations to compliment the flag of the Crown of England. Its dignity is theirs; its splendour animates them, because it is their own. And shall they suffer an Anglo-American adventurer to depreciate their own glory?

---

* See proposals of Reform in her Representation, Second Part of Rights of Man.

John

John Bull. There will be no end to his vanity while he can write ; but his reputation muſt ceaſe with every true Engliſhman who can read.

The Author. Clearly ſo, by the following citations from his book, which being written by a man who, taking him at his own words, has arrived to an eminence in political literature, the man of ſenſe will bluſh at his vague conjectures, and the politician deſpiſe his ſtrained definitions of Government. I ſhall ſelect a few from the many which occur in his laſt work *, and arrange them under the following heads :

METAPHYSICAL ABSURDITIES.

" Were even ourſolves to come again into exiſt-
" ence, inſtead of being ſucceeded by poſterity,
" we have not *now* the right of taking from our-
" ſelves, the right which would *then* be ours.

" The wretched ſtate to which man is reduced
" by wars, under eſtabliſhed Governments, is cer-
" tainly not the condition Heaven intended for
" man.

" Could it be made a decree in Nature, and
" man could know it, &c. &c.

* Second Part Rights of Man.

The

" The ridiculous infignificance into which lite-
" rature and the fciences would fink could they be
" made hereditary.

" The myfterious word Government robs in-
" duftry of its honours by *pedanticly* making itfelf
" the caufe of its effects, and purloins from the
" general character of man the merits that apper-
" tain to him as a focial being.

" The prefent generation will appear to the fu-
" ture as the Adam of a new world."

POLITICAL ABSURDITIES.

" The inhabitants of every country under the
" civilization of laws eafily civilize together. But
" Governments being yet in an uncivilized'ftate,
" and almoft continually at war, they pervert the
" abundance which civilized life produces, to
" carry on the uncivilized part to a greater ex-
" tent.

" The keeping the wild beafts in the Tower can
" be no other than to fhew the origin of Govern-
" ment ; they are in place of a Conftitution. O,
" John Bull, what honours thou haft loft by not
" being a wild beaft !

" Government

" Government has two diftinct characters. One
" civil, difpenfing laws at home; the other of the
" court, operating abroad on the rude plan of un-
" civilized life; the one attended with little charge,
" the other with boundlefs extravagance; and fo
" diftinct are the two, that if one was to fink as it
" were by a fudden opening of the earth, and to-
" tally difappear, the former would not be de-
" ranged.

" When the ability in any nation to buy is de-
" ftroyed, it equally involves the feller.

" Could the Government of England deftroy
" the commerce of all other nations, fhe would
" moft effectually ruin her own.

" The more perfect civilization is, the lefs oc-
" cafion it has for Government, becaufe the more
" does it regulate its own affairs, and govern itfelf.

" Civil Government does not confift in execu-
" tions.

" Were a Government fo conftructed, that it
" could not go on unlefs a goofe or a gander were
" prefent in the Senate, the difficulties would be
" juft as great and as real on the flight or ficknefs
" of the goofe or the gander, as if it were called a
" King."

John

John Bull. If his reputation depends on his wit, his lame attempts will deprive him of the laft remaining remnant.

The Author. His attempts, in general, facrifice his principles. For inftance, " levelling all di-
" ftinctions, equalizing property, one form of
" Government in Europe *, and univerfal peace,"
can never be accomplifhed, Governments being
fubject to all the various affections of men. Till
he can eradicate felf-love, the parent of felf-intereft from the heart, his theories will prove fallacious.
If we believe him, we might imagine, that by re-
generation * he can produce a new creation, divefted of all pofitive vices; and this new fpecies of
mortals are to kifs and be friends in every quarter
of the globe. Adam's tranfgreffion is atoned for
in the American Elyfium, and all the world is becoming an uniform paradife. Happy they who live
to fee that golden age. Pale Poverty no more fhall
diftrefs the eye of Humanity. Imperious Princes
no more to wars of plunder fhall command the affectionate hufband, breathing an heroic figh over
the dewy cheeks of a fond wife; no aged parent,
with filver hairs, fhall be brought to filent forrow
for the lofs of a dutiful fon, his prop and pillow,

* See his anticipation of all Europe becoming one Republic, Second Part Rights of Man.

† Remark the frequent ufe of this word in Rights of Man.

fnatched

fnatched by vultures to the altar of a mad ambitious
war. No more fhall polluted ftreams of vice offend the blufhing moon; all Nature fhall revel in
one long Summer's day; Heaven fhall fhower
down manna to all; wailing and gnafhing of teeth
fhall no more prevail; but an univerfal love fhall
reign, and every one fhall have an equal fhare
of manna *.

John Bull. As he is in poffeffion of the philofopher's ftone, and in his dedication to Fayette he
promifes to join him on the borders of Germany, I
fhall recommend him to lofe no time in imparting
his fecret to the French.

The Author. Your recommendation receives my
hearty concurrence. My beft wifhes attend the
rights of man in every defpotic State. Next we
proceed to notice the Ariftocratic party, at the
head of whom I find a brilliant champion. In contemplating the genius and talents of this great political character, admiration, furprize, and regret,
play on the flattered fenfes, which are alternately
animated with retrofpect and damped by dereliction. Who fo eminently diftinguifhed himfelf the
patriot hero? Who fo induftrioufly probed every

* See his chimerical fpeculations in Second Part of Rights of
Man, for equalizing property, and his philanthropic plan of
granting annuities to the poor.

canker

canket which affailed the Conftitution ? Who fo
indefatigable for public Reform ? Even from the
Eaftern Empire down to the Royal kitchen experienced the effects of his improving genius. Who
fo glorioufly laboured to reduce the overgrown influence of the Crown ? Who declaimed with more
applaufe and patriotifm during the American war?
The very Minifter himfelf trembled at his oratory,
more than Felix did when reproved by Paul.

John Bull. Alas ! the age of patriot chivalry is
no more ! The Genius of Liberty is tranfplanted
to a more propitious foil, and the Norman feeds
are vegetating. It is poffible, and I fhould rather
conclude his patriotifm became a facrifice to the
Higher Powers. The fmiles of a Court are very
tempting in the decline of a Parliamentary career.

The Author. We have fo many inftances of de-
fection in the *finale* of great political characters, as
amount to a clear proof that the Conftitution has
long fince been invaded by undue influence, which
prevents men of the greateft patriotic virtues from
meeting the reward due to their public fervices,
without fubjecting their inward fincerity to the
mafk of a corrupt fyftem. I fhall briefly notice
the chief Ariftocratic dogmas, or Tory principles,
which eclipfe the brilliant thoughts, the glowing
imagination, and deep erudition of this great politician, and that gave the alarm, and excited a
fpirit

spirit of political inveftigation, which tends to difhonour and depreciate thofe hereditary rights and
claims, which he takes an unqualified occafion to
affert. He has created a jealoufy among thofe
whom it would perhaps have been a merit in him
rather to have applauded than to have cenfured;
and notwithftanding his inimical views, he has fanned the flame for religious toleration, and effen-
tially infpired the caufe of liberty.

John Bull. It is an ill wind which blows no one
good. The prefcriptions of power oft betray the
want of wifdom. He fhould have known John
Bull never gulps a pill but by his own choice.

The Author. It is ftrange a man who has been
your advocate fo many years fhould forget your
difpofition. It is impoffible your native independent fpirit could affent to his arbitrary principles,
which in his bitter invectives againft the Diffenters
he has laid down. He is an inftance of that frailty
of human nature which all men deplore, when they
perceive a great man difplaying his abilities at the
expence of his wifdom and philofophy. Religious
difcords in a free State have the peculiar faculty,
above all other evils, to render the arm of Government defpotic. The attack on Dr. Price is for that
reafon the more inexcufable from a man of learning
and a philofopher. A few ftrictures on the particular paffage in that celebrated divine's fermon I
fhall

ſhall ſubmit to your conſideration. He obſerves *,
" That on the three following principles, and
" more eſpecially on the laſt, was the Revolution
" founded.

" The right to liberty of conſcience in religious
" matters.

" Secondly, The right to reſiſt power when
" abuſed. And,

" Thirdly, The right to chuſe our own Gover-
" nors, to caſhier them for miſconduct, and to
" frame a Government for ourſelves.

" Were it not true that liberty of conſcience is
" a ſacred right, that power abuſed juſtifies re-
" ſiſtance, and that civil authority is a delegation
" from the people. Were not, I ſay, all this
" true, the Revolution would have been not an
" aſſertion, but an invaſion of rights; not a Re-
" volution, but a rebellion."

It cannot be inferred from the above premiſes,
that Dr. Price conſiders the Crown elective. His
inferences undoubtedly are, that there exiſts a right
unalienable in the body of the people to maintain
their liberties. But on this important period I

* P. 34.

D   ſhall

shall reserve a more full discussion for your political history, and briefly observe, that as the Constitution was recovered at the Restoration, the people acquired no new rights at the Revolution, which Mr. Burke affirms Dr. Price assumes. When the contract between the King and people is broken on the part of the King, the people may withdraw their allegiance, and a Parliament may peaceably supply the defect, but it has no right to frame a new form of Government. It is the interest of every individual in the nation to have the Constitution considered inviolable.

The principles of Dr. Price are laid down on the true basis of liberty; but as they have called forth so much virulence, let me enquire of what serious import are these dogmas to you, whether asserted by an Archbishop of Canterbury, a Pope of Rome, a Doctor Sacheverel, or a Doctor Price? What ground is there to excite your prejudice, if they be consonant to the spirit of your free Constitution?

John Bull. That they are the immortal principles of freedom admits of no doubt. And as the sons of Freedom, with life and fortune we will maintain them, and with a noble pride deeming ourselves an enlightened people, we will support the established Church in its utmost purity; but we disclaim all invidious rancour with sectaries; we esteem ourselves

felves as brethren in reference to the main principles of the Gofpel. The flavifh dogmas of the
Roman church, and every fuperftitious formality,
vanifh as Reafon recovers her fovereign fway; and
all the ridiculous embargoes, and unneceffary im-
pofts on the road to Heaven, are clearly difcovered
to be the invention of priefts, who, as a worthy
fecretary obferved, " appeared to him like fo many
" pilots, who tell of a thoufand fand-banks, ob-
" ftructing the road into port, in order to be paid
" the pilotage. Scarce any thing to me is fo fafe,
" fo eafy, and fo pleafant, as the way which con-
" ducts to Heaven—Love God, love your neigh-
" bours, and be juft. This is our law and our
" prophets."

The Author. But it muft be confeffed the intemperate zeal of many divines has carried them fo far,
as to mix politics with divinity in the pulpit, and
its fatal effects have been experienced in every age.
The exprefs duty of the Clergy is to promote the
happinefs of mankind. True happinefs can only
be derived from a rigid adherence to the religious
and moral duties of life, and it is their particular
unwearied duty to enforce them. On political topics it may be a queftion, whether it be confiftent
to write as citizens, at leaft let them preach as divines. Our Saviour never made one parable on
politics; this fhould be a powerful example with
the miniftry. The union of Hierarchy and Court

intrigue

intrigue has been a bane to mankind. It is pampered pride and domineering ambition, feasted by the labour and toil of poverty and ignorance. Had our Great Politician been content to explode this heterogeneous mixture, we should have applauded the wielding of his glittering falchion; but we must wholly condemn the consequences, when we find it sheathed in the vitals of our very freedom.

John Bull. To preach infallibility in Church or State, is a gross reflection on the good sense of the age. That breaches in the Constitution will be made, and abuses insinuate themselves, are as certain as the fallibility of man.

The Author. Most assuredly; notwithstanding the chief statutes are founded on equity and reason, and the practical use of them for ages has rendered them venerable, as was remarked by the Commons at the conference with the Lords of Charles the First's reign, in the noble struggle between Patriotism and Despotism, " That the laws of Eng-
" land were grounded on reason more ancient than
" books, consisting much in unwritten customs,
" and so full of justice and true equity, that their
" most honourable predecessors and ancestors
" many times propugned them with a *nolumus mu-*
" *tari;* and so ancient, that from the Saxon times
" they had continued for the most part the same, as
" appeared

" appeared in the old remaining manufcripts of
" the laws of Ethelbert, King of Kent, and of
" Alfred, after the union of the Heptarchy."

John Bull. But have not the civil laws been
twifted, fhaped, and turned, like the Sybilline leaves,
according as chance has formed the pericraniums
of the grand interpreters, who have refined upon
refinement with the fluctuations of intereft, that in
many inftances the pandect has been tortured into
another fenfe. Is not the police as defective as
that of any State in Europe, wherein magiftrates
make a trade of juftice, and a fwarm of pettifog-
gers pick a man's pocket in open Court. And, in
like manner, the political ftatutes, have they not
been perverted by the flagitious collufions in office,
and abufe of public money? Has not the liberty
of the fubject been abufed by extra-judicial con-
ftructions on libels, and abridging the rights of
juries? And has not the political part of the Conftitution been rendered null and void by the violation of the freedom of election.

The Author. Your farcafms fet Envy at defiance.
Malice, indeed, may direct her fhafts at the fhield
of Truth, but in vain; they will recoil, to her own
deftruction.

John Bull. Thefe facts being admitted, will any
reafonable and independent man affirm this is an

improper

improper period to reform the reprefentation? When will the Meffiah come? Will he not rather fay, let us embrace a peaceful opportunity to repeal the obnoxious and oppreffive refinements of the law. Let us correct abufes in time, and render efficient the ftatute laws of the land, which are founded on true equity and reafon. Is not this the end of Government, the relative duty of Governors to the governed.

The Author. Beyond a doubt, it is the *fine qua non* of liberty. But your enemies will fay your zeal for reform difcovers a general principle, which proving too much, renders a perverfe practice the common effect. Better mitigate error than facrifice precedents.

John Bull. The law of precedents is ufeful, fo far as to afcertain the two fundamental principles, right and wrong. Sovereign regal power converts a bad precedent into a worfe practice, by appealing to precedents eftablifhed in an illiterate age. Sovereign reafon, the illuminating deity of Man for this century paft, verging into light and perception, rejects the ignorance of military ages, and, fhocked with the bloody fhield of revenge, feeks the enlightened rays of the fciences and the arts; and the wifdom of the prefent age laughs to fcorn thofe interefted few, who pretend to be panic ftruck with the idea of reforming abufes.

The

The Author. No precedent can be maintained againſt the conviction of reaſon and truth. In the hiſtory of this country, I find through every cen-tury, Prerogative, Ariſtocracy, and Prieſthood, have been alternately vigilant depredators on the rights of the great majority of people; and at dif-ferent periods it became abſolutely neceſſary for the Democratic part to oppoſe equality of right to the inequality of men, to remedy the abuſes of the Conſtitution; and it is evident that the defect and abuſe of the repreſentation of the people has been the ſole cauſe of all the grievances and innovations which have occurred ſince the Revolution. What opinion then can you entertain of a man who lays down the following unconſtitutional and dangerous dogmas.

* 1ſt. That the King holds his Crown wholly in-dependent, and in contempt of the nation.

2d. That the people of England have in no caſe whatever any more right to alter or interrupt the hereditary ſucceſſion once eſtabliſhed, than they have wholly to aboliſh the monarchy.

† 3d. That the Ariſtocratic and Democratic parts of the Conſtitution originate with, and derive all their legal power from the King.

---

* Reflections.   † Appeal, p. 46.

Hence

Hence Kings do not derive their right to the Crown from the people, and are not refponfible to them, which is a moft arbitrary dogma, denying in its confequences the very principles of our free Conftitution, which has fo wifely provided againft the fucceffion of a tyrant, by placing the fupreme power in the Legiflature, and rendering a King fubordinate to the law. We do not at firft view fee the remote confequences to which this libel on the Conftitution applies. It is a renunciation of the rights and powers of the people to legiflate for themfelves, and fets the will of the King above the law. In fact, thefe principles being equally as un-conftitutional as the Republicans, and prior in publication, whatever faction or anarchy have or may arife in confequence, this great politician * " is deeply refponfible, and an enemy to the free " Conftitution of this kingdom."

When principles fuch as the foregoing proceed from a man who has left the veffel of patriotifm, and clung to the throne, who has forfaken the true principles of conftitutional liberty, men will regard with a jealous eye the progreffive fteps of arbitrary power by the growing increafe of fecret and cor-rupt influence †.

* Sir Brooke Boothby's Obfervations, p. 73.
† What I confefs was uppermoft with me, what I bent the whole force of my mind to, was the reduction of that corrupt in-fluence which is itfelf the perennial fpring of all prodigality and

of

John Bull. I wish some learned Aristocrat would teach me the dead languages, that I may be convinced I have a living Constitution, for this secret and corrupt influence is Latin and Greek to me. In fact, the dead languages conceal many mysteries; for the other day, reflecting that too many tythe pigs found their way to the Rectors, when poor Dactyle, the Curate, looked as if he had not tasted a slice since he put on the *toga*; I took the liberty to remonstrate with the jolly ecclesiastic, who dogmatically asserted his claim in Greek; and when I enquired of Dactyle into the matter of right, the pedagogue, anticipating the parsonage, supported his Reverend Master's argument in Latin. Thank God, I replied, I am not the first man who has been talked out of his reason by Latin and Greek; neither are we the first nation. Oh, the glorious liberty of the press, I have nothing but that bulwark left to shame men into virtue, to extract from their vices, and maintain my interest in the State.

The Author. John Bull, forbear your illustrations. Let your zeal be weighed in the scale of your understanding, and then your friends will not charge

of all disorder, which loads us more than millions of debt, which takes away vigour from our arms, wisdom from our Councils, and every shadow of authority and credit from the most venerable parts of our Constitution..

Mr. Burke's Speech, Feb. 11, 1780.

you

you with a heated imagination. But as your hints apply to the neceſſity of a Reform in the mode of ſupporting the Eſtabliſhed Church, I cannot without deep concern remark its expedience, from the apparent decay of its diſcipline and ſanctity, which is occaſioned by continuing the laws of an intolerant age, at a period when time has entirely changed the face of things. In the days of ſuperſtition, the people, by the ſacrifice of a temporal property, overlooked the mercenary views of the church in the proſpect of an eternal felicity. But in this enlightened age the Clergy can hope nothing from the ſanctity of their order, when the very means of their ſupport are eſteemed by their pariſhioners as not founded in reaſon or equity. But this, John Bull, is a ſubject we ſhall leave to the wiſdom of the Legiſlature.

John Bull. Aſſuredly; but you muſt permit me to reply to the imputation of a heated imagination, and on the leading ſubject leave you to decide, when I affirm, and will maintain, that the nation of which I compoſe claims an inherent and unalienable right to preſerve the conſtituent parts of the Conſtitution independent and entire; and I utterly diſclaim any right a Parliament might claim to alter the Conſtitution, contrary to this the collective ſenſe of the community. The King, Lords, and Commons, are in truſt for themſelves and myſelf, John Bull; and whenever they ſeparate

rate

rate the joint intereft, by the Conftitution I am authorized to remonftrate; it impowers me eventually
to interfere. If the Executive Power influences a
majority in the Legiflature, our Conftitution is violated. That the venality of borough traffic, and
the effects of the Septennial Act, have repeatedly
reduced us to this dilemma, is too palpable. By
the ftern virtue of my anceftors was the path laid
down for pofterity to walk in. Let the prefent
age remember, that it ever was the difpofition of
arbitrary power to deface it; let us therefore, with
the fame native fpirit of our anceftors, unanimoufly
refolve to reclaim an equal and free delegation of
our elective power, that we may ftand upon fure
ground.

The Author. With infinite pleafure, John Bull,
I congratulate you on difcovering true Englifh fpirit. I muft confefs you have borne away the palm;
and I am proud to fay, in your dignity 1 perceive
juftice; in your firmnefs, truth; in your judgment, reafon; and in your refolution, the trio
combined.

John Bull. Reafon, truth, and juftice are the
facts we are at iffue on. Let not any man think
that with impunity he can violate thofe laws which
God has rendered facred, and equally to be enjoyed
by every individual; which are the foundation of
liberty, the rich confolation to the human mind,
the

the balmy fuccour to virtuous affliction, and the ftern reproof to vicious principles.

The Author. After fome private converfation, John Bull left me, firft engaging to renew his vifits every day till I had fully afferted his rights.

SECTION.

SECTION II.

Remarks on the Rights of Man, Society and Government.

AT this next vifit from John Bull, he very politely declined any further dialogue for the prefent, and left me to purfue thefe topics agreeable to my own inclination. Before I proceed, I may be permitted to obferve, that having differed on political points with writers of both parties, and in the courfe of my obfervations may have occafion to differ with others of not fo modern a date, I fhould incur the imputation of prefumption, if my difference of opinion went merely with a view to criticife; my chief object is the inveftigation of true conftitutional principles. And, as Voltaire has well obferved, men are fo varioufly conftituted, that fome by nature reafon wrong, others are incapable of reafoning, and others again are ever inclined to oppofe and cenfure thofe who do reafon: confeffing myfelf free, therefore, from every confideration of party prejudice or interefted motive, I fhall deliver my fentiments on political points, as reafon prefents them to my mind, and, with the greateft deference, I beg to fubmit them to the candid reader.

In

In difcuffing the fubjects of this fection, I fhall endeavour to avoid prolixity, as from an intimate acquaintance with my friend John Bull, I find, though he be poffeffed of patience to fift the few grains of corn from the chaff, he is better pleafed when he is faved the trouble.

The firft fubject which comes under our notice is the rights of man, which appears to be treated of by fome in too general a manner. When men, fpeaking of government, talk of natural rights, it pre-fuppofes a ftate of nature pre-exifting before fociety was formed. But as I do not find any author who has been able to prove a real exiftence of this primitive ftate, the rights, powers and properties of this natural ftate can be only hypothetical. To confider man in this abftracted ftate, is merely fpeculative and fallacious; for philofophers affume a maxim, where no caufe appears, it is to be confidered as not exifting. If, therefore, we fail in proving this general ftate of nature, we lay down wrong principles, by afferting natural rights in a ftate of fociety, and treating of them in abftracted terms. Adam, for the very fhort period he was by himfelf, was in a ftate of nature; and the legendary tales of Robinfon Crufoe, Philip Quarles, &c. fhew alfo they were in the fame ftate. But they were no longer in that primive ftate than when they were by themfelves. So foon as companions were added to them they entered into a ftate of fociety,
wherein

wherein their natural liberty was refigned for reciprocal benefits; an exchange of natural rights for
focial liberties took place, for which God, in a fingular manner, had fitted the human mind.   Upon
further enquiry of thefe undefined natural rights,
Mr. Locke obferves*, '' where there is no law there
'' is no freedom ;'' and where no law is there can be
no tranfgreffion.   Right is therefore reduced to a
mere legal term ; for admitting thefe maxims, it is
evident laws only can eftablifh rights ; and laws
can only arife from fociety, being rules of conduct
emanating from the reafon and confcience of men,
under a fenfe of their weaknefs, their wants, and
their fears.   And as the Holy Scripture informs
us, all men are equal in the fight of God, Blackftone, Locke, Montefquieu, and other eminent
authorities, have truly affirmed all men are equal
in focial rights ; I fay focial rights in contradiction
to natural rights ; for, upon examination, we find
when they defcend to particulars all their varied
definitions of polity bottom on one fundamental
principle, focial liberty, a renunciation of meta-
phyfical natural rights for reciprocal duties and
benefits; *man, in a focial ftate, being entitled to the
full enjoyment of every acknowledged benefit of life, he
is only reftrained from doing wrongs and committing
injuries.* Hence I conclude there is no fuch primitive ftate as that of nature, but to folitary fepa-

* On Gov. p. 2—57.

rated

rated individuals, no such unlimited power as natural right in a society of men; and I am of opinion the anarchy and riots which have arisen among the lower orders of people, have been occasioned by their not having formed certain fixed ideas of social duties and restraints; they have mingled natural and social rights together, have overlooked the reciprocal duties of social life, and by intemperate notions of natural liberty have confounded the relative obligation to submission with the undefined power of resistance, which has occasioned the most violent disorders in the community. To admit a state of nature wherein man has natural independent rights, and clash them with social restraints, is mere sophistry. Under the impression of these indiscriminate rights, a man who plunders or sets fire to another's house, is reduced to a level with the brute creation. This ideal state of nature and natural rights lessens the dignity of the human race, which God has eminently exalted above the whole creation, endowed man with reason, and " put him under strong obliga-" tion of necessity, convenience, and inclination, " to drive him into society, as well as fitted him " with understanding and language to continue " and enjoy it *." These riots and factions in society are the effects of ignorance, and frequently

* Locke on Gov. p. 2—77.

are

are the immediate caufes of neceffary laws which
border on tyranny. The beft affurance for the
higheft enjoyment of focial liberty is a general diffufion of knowledge among the lower orders of
people. When the reafon of man is directed to
true principles, it conquers more than the fword,
and is the true fource of liberty, peace, and virtue.
It is only by the ignorance of the greateft number
in a State that it wears the chains of flavery an hour.
Enlightened reafon gives an energy to the human
mind which defpots tremble at; and, like fallen
angels, fink before truth, in guilty pufillanimity
and defpair.

The next and fecond fubject of remark is Society, for which ftate man is peculiarly fitted by
his maker; and for the free enjoyment of liberty
in this ftate, men have no other rules to refort
to than the laws of Nature and revelation, which
are the laws of God. Thefe laws I fhall briefly
notice, in order to afcertain the focial duties and
rights of man. It is certain that man, by Nature fubject to the eternal and immutable laws of good and
evil, wanted not promulgated precepts to direct
him in the purfuit of his own true and fubftantial
happinefs, "* which is the bafis of the natural law."
For God endowing man with reafon, had enabled
him by the aid of his confcience to difcover the

* Blackftone's Com. vol. i. p. 41.

E

commixed

commixed principles of good and evil, and to difcriminate rules of action by which his rights, his
interests, and his happiness might be assured him.
These first principles of conduct, which secured
those benefits, and which are reciprocal in society,
were to honour God, to live honestly, to injure no-
body, to render to every one his due, and in all
things to do unto other as he would be done by.
These general precepts constitute the law of Nature.

But the reason of man being corrupt, and his
understanding full of ignorance, the exercise of
right reason was perverted by self-love, that uncultivated, yet indispensible spur, grafted on the mind
to quicken it to action, and engage it in the pursuits
of its own happiness. This occasioned the benign
interposition of the Divine Author of Nature, in
compassion for the frailties of human reason, to difcover and enforce its laws, by an immediate and
direct revelation. The doctrines thus delivered are
called the Divine Law, and they are only to be
found in the Holy Scriptures. These precepts
when revealed were, on comparison, not only found
to be a part of the original principles of the natural
law, but tending eminently to illuminate the mind,
and conduce to man's felicity.

From these Laws of Nature, and the Divine Law,
spring all human laws. To these general precepts
Justinian

Juftinian has reduced the whole doctrine of law *;
and it follows that the conftitutional law of every
State fhould be founded on thefe eternal laws of
true equity and reafon. No human laws are binding or valid if contrary to them. To eftablifh thefe
laws, and fecure their obfervance in fociety, certain
reftraints and limitations muft be impofed. Neverthelefs Mr. Blackftone obferves, the rights of
man, independent of fociety, leave him under the
Divine as well as natural law, to purfue his own
liberty agreeable to the dictates of his reafon, independent of any human laws. But fo brutifh a
ftate is incompatible with human nature, man being
incapable of living alone; neither has he refolution to live reclufe from fociety. In fine, man, as
before remarked, was peculiarly formed for fociety,
in which, for the prefervation of peace the benefits of mutual fecurity, and the quiet poffeffion of property, natural liberty and natural
right become fubfervient to civil limitations and to
moral and religious reftraints, which is a fubmiffion of the private wills of every member of fociety
to the will of one man, or of one or more affemblies of men, chofen by the common confent of
the community, and to whom the fupreme authority is intrufted. And this will of that one man,
or affemblage of men, conftitutes the Law, for
which every individual pays the price of his natural

* Inft. i. p. 3.

liberty,

liberty, by yielding a fubmiffion in return for the
benefits of having his life, liberty, and property
protected. This exchange of fubmiffion for protection arifing from a fenfe of weaknefs and neceffity, is underftood to mean the original compact of
fociety.

Natural liberty would be truly an evil, unreftrained by focial ties ; and the allurements to focial
liberty are fo great, that a State having fecured
by laws the free poffeffion of the one, enjoy in the
higheft degree the privileges of the other.

Society being neceffary for the exiftence of
the human race, it followed, from the various
feparated divifions of the earth, and other natural
caufes, that mankind muft neceffarily be divided
into many focieties, and form feparate States and
nations, independent of each other, yet from that
univerfal prevailing difpofition to traffic, a mutual
and continued intercourfe muft arife. Hence the
regulation of this intercourfe conftitutes * the law
of nations. But as thefe different States are independent of each other, and are wholly governed by
their own laws, none can affume the power of dic-
tating to the other where there is no acknowledged
fuperiority. The regulation of this intercourfe
therefore depends on mutual treaties and compacts,

* Blackftone, vol. i. p. 13.

conftructed

conftructed on thofe principles of equity and reafon, which conftitute the Law of Nature.

The affociation of mankind into different focieties being for the enjoyment of mutual liberty and
fecurity, thefe benefits can only extend to every individual by laws framed on the principles of general liberty and equal juftice, the Laws of Nature
and of God. On thefe firft principles the civil and
religious liberties of mankind are affured them;
but that men have miftaken the true principles of
Government, or thefe firft principles have been
perverted by ambitious men, and mankind, inftead
of being happy and free, have fallen into flavery,
is too evident from the number of defpotic nations
in the world. This circumftance leads to the third
fubject of remark, which is Government.

If the Mofaic account be juft, it followed that
the firft families, fo long as the diftinct ties of re-
lationfhip could be afcertained, muft have been governed by patriarchal authority; but when thofe
ties were obliterated by the increafe of mankind,
the neceffity of eftablifhing a public intereft no
doubt convened them together, the oppreffion of
the powerful over the weak muft neceffarily have
fuggefted the idea of creating a Supreme Power,
which fhould counterpoife the natural inequality of
men, by difpenfing equal juftice and equal fecurity
to all; and this idea could only arife from a pofi-

tive

tive conviction, that every individual was equally entitled to the benefits of life; and as man from simple
rules afcend to the more complex, the fupreme
power vefted in one or more for the common intereft of the whole community muft have been created by choice, it could not have been eftablifhed
but by election, when the enviable diftinctions of
wealth and luxurious refinements were unknown.
Every man having equal right, the Legiflature no
doubt was compofed of a few leading men, diftinguifhed and chofen for their abilities and wifdom,
and the executive power deputed during pleafure
to a chieftain eminent for his qualities, to conduct
their enterprizes, to lead them in war, or to prefide in their affemblies in time of peace, forming
thus a fimple Republic, in which their rules of
conduct were rather certain ufages and cuftoms
than written laws. Abfolute monarchy could not
have been the firft form of Government, the affo-
ciations of mankind being for the fole purpofe of
protecting the weak from the powerful, it is impoffible to fuppofe they would reft under the authority of a known oppreffor.

A difquifition into the dark maze of antiquity
to eftablifh this *poftulate* were to little purpofe, the
earlieft accounts in the hiftory of modern Europe
prove that the firft known Governments were republics or principalities, poffeffing a confiderable
portion of Democracy.

The

The ancient Britons, the Germans, the Gauls, and other nations, we find were in this primitive state divided into a number of tribes, or small States, under their respective Chieftains, Heretogans, Generals, or Princes, who owed their eminence entirely to their military talents, and whose powers were so far limited as to confist rather in the power of advising than commanding, for every individual was at liberty to chuse whether he would engage in any warlike enterprize or not. The earlieft accounts therefore prove, that the chief nations in modern Europe enjoyed political liberty in the moft unlimited fenfe. Of this firft native principle of Society, I fhall have further occafion to treat, in remarks on the Englifh hiftory. It may be sufficient here to obferve, that the chief nations in Europe, from the earlieft accounts, poffeffed this firft principle, Political Liberty. To affirm it was uncultivated, rude, and barbarous, is an objection of no weight. It is the birth-right of mankind; and though it has affumed different forms and figures through different ages, in the various modes of Government which have fprung from it, fome of which have totally annulled it, yet fuch inftances afford no rational argument againft its full and compleat reftitution by any community at any future age, where it has been fo furrendered or loft.

Upon enquiry into the leading caufes of nations furrendering their liberties to the arbitrary will of

one

one individual, we find in republics the popular
affemblies in general have the public good in view;
their intentions are to do that which is right and
juft, but in the execution of their powers they are
weak, and too often divided by the ambition of
enterprifing men; and through the inordinate
thirft for power, the common intereft has been repeatedly facrificed, as different parties have prevailed, which is fully exemplified in Machiavel's
hiftory of the Republic of Florence. And though
Republics have particularly diftinguifhed themfelves
from Ariftocracies and Monarchies in public virtue, public fpirit, and patriotifm, yet the divifions
and diffenfions which they have nurfed and matured, have ever rendered their executive powers
feeble and precarious; and in confequence they
have finally funk into flavifh Ariftocracies or Monarchies, which juftifies Mr. Hume's remark *,
That all anarchy is the immediate caufe of tyranny. But from the hiftory of modern Europe
we approach nearer the truth, when we affirm, that
ignorance and fuperftition have been the caufe of
the flavery of the European nations, by means of
that grand engine of Defpotifm, Papal Authority.
But at this enlightened period, anticipation may
indulge a pleafing gratification, when it is confidered that the Church of Rome was the moft powerful combination ever formed againft the autho-

* Appendix, No. 1, p. 208.

rity

rity and fecurity of civil Government, the pillar and fupport of Defpotifm, and fworn foe to the liberty of mankind. It was a ftupendous fabric of fuperftition, maintained by the private interefts of fuch a numerous and powerful clafs of people, that feemed to fet at defiance human reafon, wifdom, and virtue. But time producing all thofe changes which refult from the active fpirit of nature, loofened thofe ties by fortuitous events, which to the efforts of the human mind, appeared impregnable, and has progreffively trenched its immenfe power, which in another century may be wholly annihilated; and wherever its power has been annulled, Freedom and Toleration have been eftablifhed, have fpread and flourifhed, as in England after the Reformation, and the entire emancipation from the Papal yoke. Again, in France its power was firft weakened by the Pragmatic Sanction, further reduced by the Concordat in the fixteenth century; and now by the Revolution its power is wholly deftroyed! And however we may differ on political points, the immortal rays of liberty have emanated with unexampled fplendour. The heavenly influence of this fpirit raifes the human race to a parallel with the higher order of beings. The mind, when unfhackled from the fuperftition of prieftcraft and defpotifm, opens to the wide expanfe of dignified nature, and imagination traverfes the globe, and
                                                    explores

explores with boundlefs refearch the arcanum of
the univerfe. The Genius of Liberty, wherever
fhe prefides, is the parent of the fciences, the arts,
and literature; her principles are the pureft in nature, being founded on charity, that firft law of
Scripture, which includes all the virtues of mutual
benefits, and gives to man all the enjoyments which
flow from the fountain of all perfection. To fecure thefe ineftimable bleffings, a form of Government has been conftituted by the French, which
Time will meliorate into a permanent fyftem of focial freedom; and being now agitated like a trou-
bled fea, is occafioned by its being founded on an
excefs of liberty, a confequence naturally proportionate to the degree of oppreffion thrown off. It
followed, when new and brilliant profpects rufhed
on the public mind, and every man's breaft glowing
with the dignity of his nature, and every tongue
freely expatiating on the glorious caufe, that the
wifdom of a great and free people fhould be daz-
zled by the light of fo pure a flame, and in the
ardour of one common caufe they fhould facrifice
much at the fhrine of Liberty, rendering feeble
thofe conftituted powers which were to compact
and confolidate into a permanent fyftem—A FREE
CONSTITUTION, THE BEST AND GLORIOUS GIFT
OF HEAVEN.

In the Emperor's dominions the fame enlightened work is begun. In the year 1781 the reduction

tion of monasteries, and the reform of the ecclesi-
astics in general threw the Conclave at Rome into
such a panic, that the aged Pope himself took the
unprecedented and dangerous journey to Vienna,
in the midst of Winter, to remonstrate in person
with Joseph II. but it proved fruitless; the work
was begun by a power superior to Sovereign Pon-
tiffs; and the period is not far distant when we
may conjecture those extensive dominions will be
as free as England and France.

Nations cannot materially err in reforming their
modes of Government at a period when the light
of reason, by a general diffusion of knowledge, is
conspicuously illuminating the civilized world, in
a manner as auspicious to the common social
rights of man, as evidently conducive to an uni-
versal toleration, agreeable to the pure precepts
of the Gospel, but which Papal authority has
with all its industry so powerfully opposed, by
keeping under St. Peter's keys those holy truths,
those sacred emanations from the Deity, to en-
lighten mankind, and to spread the blessed flame
of liberty, that man from ignorance might aspire
to a true knowledge of himself, and by that knowledge explode the mysteries of priestcraft, and shake
off the fetters of slavery. The freedom of nations
and toleration are inseparable; the first expands
the mind, and the other enlarges the soul. Despotism and priestcraft, the two evil genii which

ravage the world with war and perfecution, act in mutual contact; the firft fhackles the perfon with coercive reftraints, and the other keeps the foul in conftant terror. The conjunction of thefe two defpotic powers in Spain, Portugal, Italy, and Germany, as well as the defpotifm of Pruffia, Ruffia, Sweden, &c. is fupported by an ufurped authority over the facred birth-rights of mankind, rejecting the facred principles of Liberty, the Laws of Nature and of God; they always go armed againft their fubjects, like highwaymen againft the public; fuch is the force of conviction on the human mind, when acting on wrong principles.

Several writers of the prefent day difhonour the name of Englifhmen, and difgrace the Britifh prefs, by fixing a reproach on the advocates of Liberty, whom they ftyle illuminating philofophers. But when we reflect on the rapid progrefs of literature during the laft two centuries *, is it furprifing a general diffufion of knowledge fhould difcover itfelf in opinions the moft liberal, in fentiments the moft humane; and confequently prejudices, fuperftition, and bigotted principles, yield to the mild and temperate dictates of maturing

---

* Henry VIII. made a law that all men might read the Scripture, except fervants; but no women, except ladies and gentlewomen who had leifure, and might afk fomebody the meaning. The law was repealed in Edward VIth's days.

Selden's Table Talk, p. 7.

reafon?

reafon ? Had there been a full enjoyment of the
liberty of the prefs during the reigns of the Houfe
of Tudor, and the fubfequent years, down to the
period of the unhappy civil wars, in all proba-
bility they would not have taken place. The
Star Chamber fhackled the mind, tortured reafon,
and men were left in a ftate of political and religious darknefs. But the paffions of the multitude
were fo inflamed with their native ideas of liberty,
that the very meafures adopted to keep them in reftraint and flavery, added fuel to the fmothering pile,
which poffibly might have been prevented breaking
into a flame by the freedom of the prefs, which
carries with it the important privilege of reducing
magiftrates to the limits of the law; and though it
leaves to the higher powers no choice between
their duty and their reputation, yet it teaches the
fubject no other doctrine, it leaves him no other
privilege; it is, in fine, the very life itfelf of every
free Government, and the moving principle of
whatever is great and glorious in the State. It pre-
ferves that harmony in the various inftitutions and
conftituted orders of Government which compofe
the bond of union among the people; and one
bleffing peculiarly attends this privilege, that Kings
and Princes, as well as Minifters and Officers of
the State, can never take meafures to fecure to
themfelves the fame of pofterity, without exalting
the interefts of the people; and no man, however
high his ftation, is worthy of his place, if a regard

for

for fame and reputation is not the chief motive and active principle of his mind. This renders the liberty of the prefs a rod of terror to vicious Governors. But to the truly wife patriot, the man who nobly fupports his integrity amidft furrounding fafcinating temptations, it never ceafes to record his fame ; it is a fource to gratify the moft exalted ambition; the truly great mind will have no other emulation than to merit its fair impreffion ; and fuch men whofe rule of conduct is regulated by this noble regard for recorded reputation, merit the full confidence of the nation.

SECT.

SECTION III.

The Political Hiſtory of John Bull; or, Remarks on Political Liberty under the Britons.

THE limits which I have preſcribed myſelf, and the leading ſubject itſelf under conſideration, do neither admit nor require a narrative hiſtory; I ſhall therefore confine myſelf to occaſional remarks on political liberty, from the earlieſt accounts down to the Revolution, and endeavour to form more certain ideas and determinations on thoſe acknowledged firſt principles of the Conſtitution, which we hear of in terms generally looſe and undefined. Of theſe we muſt remark the following. The Majeſty of the People—The Sovereignty of the People—The Supreme Power of the People, &c. I ſhould imagine it to have fallen within the obſervation of moſt men, that, from the variety of ideas formed of theſe firſt principles, has ariſen the ſpirit of faction and the name of party; and the violence of different parties, which has at times both agitated and alarmed the State, proves in moſt inſtances, that particular intereſts rather than reaſon have directed their views, and private motives rather than truth have fixed their principles, of which ſome militate againſt the texture and genius

of

of our Conftitution, and others deny to the people the right of political liberty. Hence political truths, though fimple in themfelves, have acquired an elaborate mode of difcuffion; and where it has failed, or even fucceeded in elucidating fome truths, the mind has been left with faint ideas of firft principles, and the common terms Majefty of the People, &c. have become rather bombaftic popular founds than certain defined co-active powers. In difcuffing thefe firft principles, it is neceffary that circumfpection fhould guide the pen of truth; and that they may be freely difcuffed is the particular privilege of every Briton, a privilege he enjoys from poffeffing political liberty, which can never be furrendered or loft, but with the deftruction of that free Conftitution which has fprung from this firft native principle.

The Conftitution therefore growing out of political liberty, to treat of the one before we have proved the exiftence of the other is taking the effect before the caufe.—A very material diftinction occurs to my mind between Social Liberty, Political Liberty, and Civil Liberty. This diftinction, if rightly confidered, acquires an importance which I find feldom attended to by many political writers, who in general exprefs Political and Civil Liberty in fynonimous terms, and involve the general principles of the fupreme power of the people with the inftitutions and laws created by a delegated authority.

rity. With fubmiffion I make a diftinction of
thefe three defcriptions of liberty.

Social Liberty is the pofitive birth-right of mankind, without diftinction of perfons. This privilege in a State may be diftinguifhed by two general
abfolute rights; firft, the right of enjoying all
thofe benefits which are fuppofed to belong to man
in the hypothetical ftate of nature; and which,
when he enters into fociety he is permitted to retain, for the reafon that the enjoyment of them
does not interfere with the interefts or happinefs of
any of his fellow-creatures. By thefe abfolute
rights a man enjoys *loco* motion, or the power of
moving his perfon wherever his inclination leads
him, without reftraint; he likewife enjoys the privilege of living as he thinks proper; of following
his bufinefs, his pleafures, and his purfuits, agreeable to his own will, without being dictated to by
any other perfon or power whatever. Hence his
vices are not cognizable in Society, unlefs he pub-
lifhes them. A man, for inftance, may indulge in
liquor without reftraint; but if when intoxicated
he interferes with the interefts or the peace of
others, and commits injuries, he then becomes
fubject to thofe rules or laws by which the fociety
hath agreed to be governed; and that power which
every State or Society affumes of eftablifhing fuch
rules and laws, is the fecond abfolute right which
every individual is entitled to from Social Liberty.

F

And

And this right is that of Political Liberty, which is the first operative principle of fociety, and which gives to every member of a State the right of convening, either in perfon or by reprefentative, to eftablifh inftitutions and rules of conduct by which juftice fhall protect the virtuous from the vicious, the weak from the powerful, and liberty, peace, and happinefs, be enjoyed by the great majority of the community, the happinefs of the greateft number being the firft object of law in fociety. The various inftitutions hence eftablifhed form a Conftitution, and the rules and regulations laid down compofe the law or Civil Liberty, from which a material diftinction arifes between Political and Civil Liberty. Mr. J. Blackftone tells us *, " Civil Liberty leaves the fubject entire mafter of " his own conduct, except in thofe points wherein " the public good requires fome directions or re-" ftraints." From the diftinction neceffary to difcriminate between fupreme and fubordinate power, it appears evident to me, that the afcertaining thofe points, and giving directions, or creating reftraints, is the fole province of political liberty. Such reftraints, directions, or points, when expreffed and publifhed, compofe the civil liberties of the fubject, political liberty being the power and fcience of governing; civil liberty the means ufed for government; from which I conclude political liberty

* Vol. I. p. 126.

appertains

appertains invariably to social liberty, and civil liberty grows out of political liberty. These propositions induce me to make a further remark on a
passage in the Commentaries, where I find political
and civil liberty used synonimously. It is to the
following effect: " * The idea and practice of this
" political or civil liberty flourish in their higheſt
" vigour in these kingdoms, where it falls little
" short of perfection, and can only be loſt or de-
" ſtroyed by its *owner*, the Legiſlature." Though
with pleaſure we admit the premiſes, it does not
follow that the concluſion be juſt; for political liberty, or the ſupreme ſocial power, invariably re-
ſides in the body of people; and the ſupreme created power is ſubordinate to that in fact, but not
in terms. The people are the *owners* of the eſtate;
the Legiſlators are only the truſtees, and poſſeſs
not an arbitrary and diſcretionary power. But the
uſurpation of this power by the conſtituted and delegated authority of this country, ſtands recorded
on the face of hiſtory as the cauſe of all internal
commotions and civil wars. That Houſe of Commons which enacted its own exiſtence from three
to ſeven years is an inſtance the moſt violent and
arbitrary that has been exerciſed ſince the being of
a Parliament. The admiſſion and ſufferance of
that uſurpation on political liberty, has tarniſhed
the glory of every ſubſequent reign. On this ſub-

ject I shall have much to advance. It is neceffary here to form juft ideas on political liberty, before any remarks be made on its firft exiftence in this country, and its fubfequent progrefs. I shall not contract my arguments by narrow notions and prejudices, being convinced, that to liberality of fentiment we owe many bleffings; and though it be the pride of human nature to difdain fervile imitations, it is to the honour of it to diffipate prejudice, and notice with the cool eye of wifdom the virtues of the moft malignant enemy. Far be it from me to excite invidious comparifons. Truth can be only eftablifhed by elucidation; and without offering the French Conftitution by any means as an example to us, I embrace an inftance which fully eftablifhes my pofitions, and confirms the diftinction fuggefted between political and civil liberty. The French have afferted moft explicitly the common right of mankind to political liberty, and have made a very evident diftinction between that power and civil liberty, by limiting the fitting of any future National Affembly to two years, and denying to fuch Affembly the powers of continuing in its delegated capacity beyond that period, without a violent ufurpation of the conftitutional rights of the people, the rights of a nation being abfolute, the rights of an Affembly or Parliament relative. Hence political liberty is an abfolute power, which the body of people at any future age may affume,

to

to remedy the abuses of civil liberty, which is a subordinate, created, and relative privilege.

The origin of Constitutions and the various modes of Government being antecedent to all records, we have no lights to guide us through the dark maze of antiquity, by which we can trace their first principles, but the exercise of our reason, aided by those accounts of ancient Government which are known, and which antiquity hath rendered venerable. Many eminent writers, distinguished for their learning, incur the suspicion of narrow minds or biassed principles, when they affect to pass over the first æra of the British history, as a maze where perspicuity would be trammelled with defaced pictures, and truth itself be lost in the research. This disregard to antiquity is attended with effects which fully prove an unwarrantable industry to accommodate facts to principles. It may be useful and entertaining to read the laws, institutions, and customs of our ancestors; but when men strain at the precise meaning of an old law, attempt to refute the existence of a particular institution, quibble about the word conquest, depreciate the *poor* Commons, and affirm that the representation of the people arose from the grace and favour of Norman despots. It is with pain, mingled with indignation, we see men of superior abilities and learning disgracing in this

F 3 manner

manner the annals of liberty, by drowning her genius in the vortex of law.

To engage in the controverfy between popular
and monarchical writers would be foreign to my
purpofe ; I fhall endeavour, by unqueftionable authority to confirm the pofition, that political liberty
invariably refides in the body of people, independent of any refinements of law or religion; and
that from the earlieft accounts of antiquity, its co-
active powers have been enforced, and may at all
times be exercifed by the majority of the community, when the injuftice and oppreffion of its delegated powers demand the common intereft to be
preferved.

The rude hiftory of ancient Britain affords no
flattering topic for an hiftorian, no inftruction for
the reader. The higheft gratification which an
Englifhman can derive are thofe well authenticated
records, which prove, that the Britons enjoyed political liberty. To confult thofe remote æras with
an eye prejudiced by modern political refinement, leads to error and party. The refinement of
manners was wholly unknown in thofe early periods
of fociety; thofe nice diftinctions between the principles Right and Wrong ; and thofe *wire-drawn*
decifions in our modern courts of juftice could
only be attained by the refinement of many centuries.

ries. The mind therefore ought to be prepared for the diftinction between a military age, when the virtues of valour, the love of liberty and independence, were carried to the higheft pitch, and that of a commercial age, when wealth creates enviable diftinctions, and a thirft of gain facrifices every noble principle of the mind. Men who make this neceffary diftinction between the two ages, contemn the narrow and dark controverfy, whether the Britons were governed by abfolute Monarchs or enjoyed Republics, whether their Kithifrins *commune confilium regni*, or Parliaments, were compofed of Commoners or Peers, or whether they enjoyed a limited Monarchy. If we can gather from approved authority that they enjoyed the common right of mankind, political liberty, however bold, fierce, or unrefined, the argument will be compleat. And when our anceftors at the Revolution, in their Declaration claim, demand, and infift upon all and fingular the premifes as their undoubted rights and liberties, and 1 Wm. and Mary, f. 2. cap. 2. recognizes all and fingular the rights and liberties afferted in the faid Declaration to be the true, ancient, and indubitable rights of the people of this kingdom; and the Act of Settlement, which again confirms thefe liberties, declares them to be the birth-right of the people of England, where fhall we fix the æra for thefe inheritances, if we do not eftablifh them from the remoteft antiquity. If the Revolutionifts ran over the ftring of

periods

periods or data, where would they stop, or where
shall we now stop? The Petition of Right, the
thirty-two corroborating statutes of the two Charters, the Magna Charta itself, and all the Charters
granted, or obtained sword in hand from Norman
despots, without equivocation declare the premises
insisted on to be the ancient rights and liberties of
the people of England. What the express verbal
liberties of Edward the Confessor were, History
does not fully explain *. We find by Mr. Hume
some antiquaries as well as himself have narrowed
their ideas, and political liberty hath suffered in
the research for express laws; but these laws of
Edward the Confessor, we learn, were merely confirmations of those established by Alfred; we may
therefore presume they were nothing less than those
great outlines of political liberty which that wise

---

* What these laws were of Edward the Confessor which the
English, every reign during a century and a half, desire so pas-
sionately to have restored, is much disputed by Antiquaries, and
our ignorance of them seems to be one of the greatest defects in
ancient English History. The collection of laws by Wilkins,
which pass under the name of Edward's, are plainly a posterior
and an ignorant compilation. Those to be found in Ingulf are
genuine, but so imperfect, and contain so few clauses favourable
to the subject, that we see no great reason for their contending
for them so vehemently. It is probable the English meant the
common law as it prevailed during the reign of Edward, which
we may conjecture to have been more indulgent to liberty than
the Norman institutions. The most material articles of it were
afterwards comprehended in Magna Charta. Vol. I. p. 479.

man.

man had digefted from Saxon and Britifh originals, and which were involved in the two charters which partially comprize thofe ancient rights and liberties, fo firmly and fo effectually infifted on. The laws and inftitutions of the Great Alfred, Hiftorians inform us were improvements on the cuftoms and ufages of the Germans and Britains ; and the native Britons, it will appear, poffeffed fuch a confiderable portion of Democracy, that they may truly be faid to enjoy political liberty. And here, to ufe the expreffion of another, our enquiries find a refting place, our reafon finds a home.

From the preceding remarks it appears, political liberty muft be taken in its general fenfe, meaning the operative power of the people collectively, or by delegation affembled, to maintain the common intereft and happinefs of the great majority of the nation. But in every age civil liberty, which is its effect, will conftantly affume the fafhion of the reigning day ; and laws which were neceffary and beneficial in one age, and to that age appeared to be formed according to ftrict right and juftice, by a future age may be deemed unjuft and oppreffive; the inference follows, that the particular inftitutions and laws of remote ages are only ufeful to the prefent age, as in the fcale of common right juftice fhall incline the balance, fo truly fluctuating are human affairs.

The

The chief writers among the ancients from whom we learn the beft accounts of the ancient Britons are Cæfar and Tacitus; their authority has in general obtained the confidence of all hiftorians. By Cæfar's Commentaries, it appears the Britons were divided into a number of fmall States, in which Democracy had the afcendant. On his invafion, he exprefly tells us *—" Among the Britons the " chief command and adminiftration of the war " was, by the Common Council, beftowed on " Caffivelan." And that the Commons were called to this Affembly, Sothilius † fays the commonalty compofed a chief part in their public councils. Other corroborating teftimonies I fhall deduce, to prove that the Britons enjoyed the common right of mankind, political liberty. Milton, the immortal bard, in his Hiftory of Ancient Britain, refers to all the known ancient authors, and from his undoubted veracity two inftances may be felected, which are ftrong evidences of the exiftence, at that epoch, of this true native fpirit of liberty, which is fo much the pride and glory of Englifhmen. Britain at the period of the Roman Invafion was divided into feparate States, indepen-

* Lib. V. c. 5.
† Mr. Juftice Doddridge on the Antiquity of Parliaments, p. 66. who cites Francis Tate—*Apud bos papulus magna ex parte primatum tenet:*—Alfo Vitus in Hift. Brit. Lib. VIII. p. 11. Beda, Lib. II. c. 2. & 13.

dent

dent of each other; many of which had furrendered, or were subdued by the Romans, who were particularly desirous of introducing their laws and customs; for this purpose, " Cogidinus *, a Bri-
" tish King, their fast friend, had certain cities
" given him ; a haughty craft which the Romans
" used, to make Kings the servile agents of en-
" slaving others." The Silures, one of the British States, had for several years held out against the Roman yoke under their Prince Caractacus, but were at length subdued in a pitched battle on the west edge of Shropshire, before the commencement of which this valourous Prince went up and down, animating his officers and leaders †, " That this
" was the day, this was the field, either to defend
" their liberties, or to die free; calling to mind
" his glorious anceftors, who drove Cæfar, the
" Dictator, out of Britain."

This is an inftance which the modern refined spirit of liberty cannot surpafs, and shews how deeply independence and common right are rooted in the British heart. The second inftance corroborates this idea. After the victory of the Romans over Boadicea, " Suetonius ‡, the Roman
" General, gave too much way to his anger against

---

* Milton's Hift. Brit. Book II. p. 68 & 69. Tacitus Vit. Agricola.
† Milton's Hift. Brit. B. II. p. 81.   ‡ Tacitus Vit. Agricola.

" the

" the Britons, Claffician therefore fending fuch
" word to. Rome, that thefe fevere proceedings
" would beget an endlefs war, Polyclitus, no Ro-
" man, but a courtier, was fent by Nero to fee
" how things went. He admonifhing Suetonius
" to ufe more mildnefs, *awed* the army, and to
" the Britons gave matter of laughter, *who fo much*
" *even till then were nurfed up in their native liberty,*
" as to wonder that fo great a General, with his
" whole army, fhould be at the rebuke and or-
" dering of a Court fervitor."

I fhall conclude the inveftigation of that theorem
of ancient Britifh right, *Political Liberty,* by citing
a learned modern writer, who obferves *, " No-
" thing is worfe founded than an opinion induf-
" trioufly propagated by many writers, who ne-
" glecting reafon and hiftory, and guided only by
" prejudice, have afferted †, the firft government
of

---

* Dr. Stuart's Antiquity of the Englifh Conftitution. Part I.
p. 52.

† See Brady's Anfwer to Petyt, Filmer's Patriarchia, and
other writings for prerogative. The writers on this fubject feem
to confound the firft ftate of the Britons with that in which
they afterwards appeared, when conquered by the Romans.
Tacitus fays exprefsly, *Ipfi Britanni delectum, ac tributa et in-
juncta imperii numera inpigne obeuut. Si injuriæ defint, hos ægre
tolerant jam domiti ut pareant nondum ut ferviant ægri,* c. 13. And
Dion on Xiphilin, in the Life of Severus, obferves to the fame
purpofe, *Apud Britannos populus magna ex parte primatum tenet.*
The

" of the Britons was regal and defpotic, an opi-
" nion from which they infer the abfurdeft confe-
" quences. When the ambition however, or ava-
" rice of Cæfar had brought him to our ifland,
" and fucceeding Emperors were fired with the
" glory of fubjecting it to their arms, the inhabi-
" tants loft their liberty and independence.

The feveral inftances here adduced, from many
to the fame purpofe, evidently fhew, that the Britons fully enjoyed political liberty. And it is ob-
fervable from the earlieft accounts of various nations, before the purfuits of commerce and the re-
fining of manners took place, equality of right, liberty, and independence, were as well underftood
and maintained as at the prefent day. Military
valour was the peculiar excellence of an age when
liberty difcovered herfelf in great and magnanimous
enterprizes, before commerce had influenced the
minds of men to a mean hypocrify, and all the
little arts of trade had ftifled every noble effort of

The writers juft now referred to, by endeavouring to found the
Royal Prerogative fo high, think to prove, that the liberty we
enjoy was derived from the conceffion of our Monarchs. But
allowing that the ancient Britons were fubject to the arbitrary
will of Kings; that this was alfo the cafe with the Anglo-
Saxons; that William was a conqueror; and that the power of
the people leffened the defpotifm, and detracted from the dignity of our Kings, can it yet be fuppofed that their conceffions
would form a Conftitution fo wife and confiftent in all its parts
as that of England?

the

the foul. Mankind in the grofs were ever the fame. The happinefs enjoyed in thofe remote periods was no doubt equal to that of the prefent. The ancient Britons painting fuch part of their bodies as was expofed, was as elegant, fafhionable, and bewitching to them, as the tinfel gaudy trappings of the moderns. The vanity, as Milton obferves, is only removed from the fkin to the fkirt. And their mode of fighting in chariots drawn by horfes, argues, in my humble opinion, fuch a knowledge of mechanifm, as in no wife correfponds with the very barbarous and ignorant ftate fome writers reprefent them. Mr. J. Blackftone tells us *, " of a ftrong affinity and refemblance " between their tenets and difcipline and fome of " our modern doctrines of Englifh law." No inference can be drawn to the prejudice of political liberty from their rude ftate, or our ignorance of their exprefs laws and Government. When we perceive the great outlines of freedom, the love of liberty and independence pervading all ranks of people, and difcovering itfelf on all important occafions, and which the remnant of the Britons, after the Saxons had eftablifhed themfelves in England, carried with them into Wales, we are bound to yield to hiftory and reafon, and pronounce the ancient Britons, the aborigines of this ifland, FREEMEN, who fully enjoyed political liberty,

* Vol. IV. p. 408.

that

that peculiar birth-right of Englifhmen, which was
fo glorioufly exercifed in obtaining *Magna Charta*
in reviving the ancient Conftitution at the reftoration of Charles II. and the further fecuring it at
the Revolution. This privilege of convening to
maintain the free operation of the Conftitution, and
the common intereft, is the fupreme power of the
people ; a moft facred, invaluable right, growing
out of the common equality of original fociety ; a
right which every Englifhman being truly fenfible
of, will unite in the fentiment of Lord Bolingbroke, when he fays ⓔ, " I feel a fecret pride in
" that I was *born a Briton*, when I confider that
" the Romans, thofe mafters of the world, main-
" tained their liberty little more than feven cen-
" turies, and that Britain, which was a free nation
" feventeen hundred years ago, is fo at this hour."

ⓔ Remarks Hift. England; p. 66,

SECT.

SECTION IV.

Remarks on Political Liberty under the Saxons and Normans.

IN the preceding Section, I have endeavoured to imprefs on the mind the force and importance of this general axiom, That the fupreme power of the people, operating by political liberty, which is the right and power of the majority of the nation to convene at all times and feafons for the prefervation of the common intereft, is *the firft principle of Government.* With this foundation of all we hold moft facred and valuable in our Conftitution, we are well prepared to trace the progrefs of Liberty through the mazes of Superftition, the ufurpations of Defpotifm, or the crooked paths of Anarchy. With this principle the mind penetrates with the eyes of Argus—The ftern fophiftry of tyrants, the jefuitical impofitions of priefts, and the plaufible quibbles of lawyers, their rights, their powers, their privileges, and their precedents, as fhoals in a fhallow rapid current, make a great noife, but when the deep tide of reafon and common right overflows, they become filent as the grave.

We

We now enter on thofe periods of hiftory from which were derived the great outlines of our Conftitution. I fhall pafs over all thofe events and circumftances which ferve rather to amufe the mind than illuftrate the fubject we are upon, and confine my remarks to a few important points which are applicable and ufeful.

The Saxons who came over from Germany, after the dereliction of the Romans from Britain, brought with them their laws and form of Government, which has been acknowledged by all impartial writers to have been a true model of freedom; and though we are apt to conclude, in fuch early periods the purpofes of fociety were little underftood or valued, * it is however among nations whom we difgrace with the appellation of barbarous, that the duties of the citizen are moft generally known. In fine, the very form of our Conftitution, its feveral inftitutions and laws, are merely refinements on the laws and cuftoms of the Saxons, among whom political liberty feems to have been fo well underftood, that every man who held a refponfible fituation in the State was elected thereto by the body of people. The inferior civil and military officers were chofen within the feveral counties or diftricts, but their Princes, Heretogans or Generals, were elected in the public council of the nation †; in which

---

* Dr. Stuart's Ant. Eng. Conft. p. 273.　† Ib. p. 243.

every

every freeman affembled in perfon, or voted for
the reprefentative of his diftrict. In thefe national
affemblies a perfect equality reigned, but thofe only
who were diftinguifhed for their military valour
and eloquence were elected to the moft important
offices of Government. Here they alfo deliberated
about war and peace, and concerted the plan of
operation for the year, which gave rife to the annual Parliaments eftablifhed in the reign of Edward III.

From thefe Saxon originals our prefent Conftitution received its faireft outlines. The Genius of
Liberty dictated the act, and the great Alfred impreffed on the ifland of Britain thofe inftitutions
which are now become congenial with the foil.
Of Alfred we are told *, " he was a complete mo-
" del of that perfect character, which, under the
" denomination of a fage or wife man, the philo-
" fophers have been fond of delineating rather as
" a fiction of their imagination than in hopes of
" ever feeing it reduced to practice."

✝ " His mighty genius prompted him to un-
" dertake a moft great and neceffary work, which
" he is faid to have executed in as mafterly a
" manner, no lefs than to new model the Confti-
" tution, to rebuild it on a plan that fhould en-

* Hume, Hift. Eng. vol. I. p. 90. † Black. Com. vol. IV. p. 410.

" dure

" dure for ages, and out of its difcordant materials
" to form one uniform and connected whole. This
" he effected, by reducing the whole kingdom
" under one regular and gradual fubordination
" of Government, wherein each man was anfwer-
" able to his immediate fuperior for his own con-
" duct and that of his neareft neighbour's; for to
" him we owe that mafter-piece of judicial polity
" the fubdivifion of England into tithings and hun-
" dreds, if not into counties, all under the influ-
" ence and adminiftration of one fupreme magi-
" ftrate, the King; in whom, as in a general re-
" fervoir, all the executive authority of the law
" was lodged, and from whom juftice was dif-
" perfed to every part of the nation by diftinct,
" yet communicating ducts and channels, which
" wife inftitutions have been preferved for near a
" thoufand years *unchanged*, from Alfred's to the
" prefent time."

Of thefe inftitutions ordained by Alfred, the
trial by a jury of twelve men is reprefented as
" * an inftitution admirable in itfelf, and the beft
" calculated for the prefervation of liberty and the
" adminiftration of juftice that ever was devifed
" by the wit of man."

The firft principles of our Conftitution, as at
this period laid down, operated by election, the

---

* Hume, vol. I. p. 94.

only true bafis of freedom. Every ten houfeholders chofe one from among themfelves to prefide over them, and reprefent them in the fuperior courts; in which magiftrates, both civil and military, were elected for their feveral diftricts, and who alfo reprefented the whole body of people in the General Affembly of the Nation, which General Affembly, Wittena Gemote, or Meeting of Wife Men, conftituted the Saxon Parliament, which Alfred * ordained for a perpetual ufage fhould be held at London twice a year, or oftener if need be, to treat of the Government of God's people, how they fhould keep themfelves from fin, fhould live in quiet, and fhould receive right. The noble fimplicity of thefe laft lines conveys a juft idea of this good and wife man.

The executive power of the Saxons being placed in the hands of one man, who was the Sovereign, the Conftitution was partly monarchical. But as the King could not make laws without the confent of the principal men of the nation, it was in fome degree ariftocratical; and as the magiftrates of the town and rural tithings, and the counties were fummoned to the General Affembly of the kingdom, it poffeffed alfo a confiderable fhare of Democracy.

The Conftitution Alfred thus eftablifhed from Britifh and Saxon materials was a true limited Mo-

* Mirror of Juftices, Chap. I. f. 3. p. 6.

narchy, which having through a feries of fubfequent
years experienced many and dangerous viciffitudes,
the dangers it has met renders it the more venerable,
and at this period each feels an equal intereft in
the prefervation of its facred parts, as well as an in-
dignant contempt of all its enemies, both Republicans who are overtly attacking it, and Ariftocrats
who are fecretly undermining it.

It may be ufeful here to recur to the diftinction
between political and civil liberty; for when Mr.
J. Blackfton as above tells us, that the inftitutions
eftablifhed under Alfred have been preferved unchanged for near a thoufand years, we are apt to
conclude, that the nation poffeffed invariably thofe
liberties ; but when we find that William the Conqueror, by the aid of prieftcraft, rendered the Government defpotic, yet thofe inftitutions ftill re-
remained. The diftinction between civil and political liberty is rendered evident, and illuftrates
the maxim of Montefquieu, That the fubject may
be free and not the Conftitution, which I imagine
to imply, that the people may have right done
them in certain relative matters, as one individual
to another ; and in this refpect the fubject may be
partially free, and enjoy civil liberty; but having
no voice or vote in public meafures, nor fhare in
the motions of Government, which being entirely
at the arbitrary will of a King and his Council;
the Conftitution is not free, and the fubject is de-

prived

prived of political liberty. Similar ideas I fhould
conclude induced Lord Clifford, Prime Minifter of
Charles II. to fay, That if the King would be firm
to himfelf, he might carry the Government to what
height he would; for if men were undifturbed of
their properties, and were affured of liberty of confcience, and ftrict juftice done them at Weftminfter, and the army made firm to the King, there
were none that would have either will, opportunity,
or power to refift. That Charles had much at
heart the grand object of reigning defpotic, is a
fact too well confirmed. But the old Britifh fpirit
at that period was too prevalent to induce him to
hope for fuccefs by direct overt attempts. Charles
fell on the only expedient to deceive the jealous
eye of Britons, impofe on their credulity, and render
the generous bias of their difpofitions the only enemy to their real interefts. This Charles completely
effected by fecret and corrupt influence.

Without the violent example of the Conqueror,
it may be remarked, that Monarchs at a more refined period have made ufe of two methods to render
themfelves abfolute over a free people; one method,
as practifed by the late King of Sweden, by over-
awing the Diet, and by the ftern abufe of his prerogative fubjecting it to his will, which was an open,
direct, and arbitrary ufurpation of political liberty.
The fecond method, as practifed by Charles II. like
a man of gallantry, by art and addrefs corruptly influencing

fluencing the reprefentatives of the people, in order
to govern by his own will. Both methods, in their
effects, tending to one point, arbitrary power,
though widely differing in the means adopted. Of
the two methods, the firſt is open, manly, and becoming, a military hero panting with ambition for
miſtaken glory. The ſecond method is indirect,
ſecret, hypocritical, and treacherous, deluding the
people with the faireſt intentions, at the ſame time
undermining their deareſt intereſts.

Theſe reflections furniſh ſufficient evidence of
the inſtability of all Governments; the reſtleſs
aſpiring nature of man ever tends to break the
great chain of connexion which links the order of
ſociety, and ever ſubverts the beſt inſtitutions,
when operating in the minds of vicious men in
power. Hence we find the free Conſtitution of
the Saxons, at various times, tending to anarchy,
and at other periods to an actual Ariſtocracy, to
which it ſeemed inclining when the Conqueror
made his invaſion, which event overthrew the
Saxon free Government, and eſtabliſhed on its
ruins for a time a ſyſtem of civil and religious ſla-
very. The Saxons, until this combination of William and the Pope, had acknowledged the primacy
of the See of Rome, but had hitherto maintained
an independence in their eccleſiaſtical adminiſtration, and reſiſted the exorbitant claims which
ſupported the grandeur of the Papacy. Theſe were

ſufficient

fufficient motives to induce the Pope to fupport William's fucceffion to the throne of England; and it further aided his plan of church government, which was widely diffufing itfelf at this æra over Europe; for wherever civil or religious independence was eftablifhed, the heavenly powers of the Pope were thundered forth with accumulated virulence. His Holinefs efpoufed William's caufe, and by a crufade openly announced his tyrannic intentions; and as a fymbol of his Chriftian-like motives, and his charity to mankind, made William a prefent of a confecrated ftandard, with a golden *Agnus Dei*, and a ring with one of St. Peter's hairs in it; and further to promote his holy purpofes, and in order that every man might worfhip the Duke as the champion of the church, pronounced Harold a perjured ufurper, and then iffued his divine mandates, that he would excommunicate every one that oppofed William; and thus, as Mr. Hume obferves *, were all the ambition and violence of that invafion covered over fafely with the broad mantle of religion.

That the Crown of England till this period was elective, is evident by the choice made by the Wittena Gemote of Harold, who by that Affembly of the nation was fettled on the throne prior to the invafion made by William. Had the fucceffion been indifputably eftablifhed by hereditary defcent,

* Vol. I. p. 186,

Edgar Atheling, the right heir to the Crown, as son of Edmund the Outlaw, and grandson of King Edmund Ironside, would have succeeded to the throne, and been confirmed in it without doubt by the Wittena Gemote.

A few reflections arise from this circumstance on the advantages and disadvantages of the Chief Magistrate being elected by the nation, or succeeding by hereditary descent. We find, in whatever State the Crown, or Chief Magistrate, has been elective, that State has proved the theatre of anarchy; the improving wisdom of ages has taught men the ideal and dangerous power of the multitude's choosing a master; and as the science of Government becomes better understood, a true limited Monarchy approaches nearest to that perfection of civil government which both preserves the social equality of men and the common interest of all. The executive power being placed in the hands of one by hereditary descent, subject to the law enacted by the delegated authority of the people, the acknowledged right and superiority of birth embraces popular opinion, and confidence, prevents invidious distinctions, and renders faction silent. Let any one reflect on the private feelings and conviction of the two characters—a King elect or an usurper, and a King in a limited monarchy by descent, and judge from the harmony or discord of their minds, whether in general their situation be agreeable to

that

that order and tranquillity which is the essence of every community. The first, perhaps, owes his eminence to a majority opposed to a powerful candidate at the head of a faction, or may have usurped the throne. In either case their jealousies and apprehensions will be the same; their fears are incessantly suggesting to their minds the idea of assassination or poison, they continually go armed against their subjects, and seldom go or return the same road, or sleep often in the same chamber. Strangers to the blissful harmony of a smiling family, their stern brow can never relax to the enjoyments of private life, and they foster two of the greatest enemies to human happiness, jealousy and suspicion; they are never free from those miserable attendants. On the contrary, see the reverse of all this in a King by hereditary descent in a limited Monarchy, whose rule of conduct is prescribed by the legislative power of the people. If any public grievances, or any oppression on the common interest is made, or any violent abuse of the executive power is exercised, the representatives of the people have full power to redress such abuses of the constitutional rights of the people, by impeaching and punishing the Ministers and evil counsellors of the King; and this inestimable privilege must impress on the minds of all, the sacred importance of the freedom of election. In fine, to all candid inquirers, the independence of a House of Commons must appear the only bulwark of all which the

people

people hold moſt dear and valuable. The Miniſters of the Crown being reſponſible for the abuſes
of the Executive Power, a confidence ariſes be-
between King and people, which diſcovers itſelf
by a conduct of generous regard and affectionate
conduct on the part of the King, and by a grateful ſubmiſſion and ſtanch loyalty on the part of
the people ; a hereditary King in a limited Monarchy thus enjoys all the bleſſings of private life
as a man, and all the dignity and power in public
life as a King. Theſe enjoyments a King can only
aſſure to himſelf by making the intereſts of the
people his greateſt happineſs. His inceſſant duty
is to promote that order and tranquillity in a State
which is the firſt and chief object of Government.

To theſe advantages of hereditary ſucceſſion in a
limited Monarchy, I am prepared for the objections which have afforded much ſportive ridicule
to a Republican, who has wilfully overlooked the
great line of connexion which links the mutual
dependences of the Conſtitution, or he has imbibed falſe notions of its principles. But as political liberty is the ſubject of inveſtigation, the Conſtitution we ſhall notice in a future Section, and
ſhall briefly remark, that a King being a minor or
an ideot, the firſt of which has not occurred for
near two hundred and fifty years, are objections of
no weight, when it is conſidered an independent
Parliament, as preſcribed by the Conſtitution, is

ever

ever adequate to all fortuitous events of that nature. If the reprefentatives of the people be faithful, the Conftitution can never fuffer by fuch
events; limits are prefcribed to each conftituent
part, and a. violation of thofe boundaries is an
ufurpation on the rights of the people. At the
prefent period, as I fhall have occafion to obferve,
the Conftitution cannot be materially violated;
without a general fenfe of the perverfion diffufing
itfelf through all ranks, one opinion will be formed,
and one general fentiment prevail; the people will
exercife their birth-right, political liberty, and will
reftore that which they founded; the Conftitution
will acquire additional purity, and the proof of its
excellence will confift in the harmony and energy
of its powers.

From the Invafion down to the Revolution, I
fhall endeavour to be as concife as the leading fubject will admit. The treacherous conceffions which
William made after the battle of Haftings were
merely to pave his way to the Crown by the feeming confent of the Englifh nation; through the influence of the Clergy he obtained this point, but to
the infinite mortification of the Englifh, they foon
found themfelves profcribed, their eftates confif-
cated, oppreffive exactions and arbitrary laws enforced, and their native language fupplanted by the
impofition of a foreign one. Power and property
were thus united in the hands of a few, while the
multitude

multitude were deprived of their common rights. To reftore the balance of power and the balance of property was the after-work of ages. The firft circumftance that led to this equilibrium, which is the bafis of the Conftitution, was the exercife of political liberty under King John. The regaining of this facred principle of primeval right will ever command the feelings and infpire the mind with the true principles of liberty. When the Executive Power exceeds the limits of juftice, and ufurps a tyranny which reafon renounces and freedom difclaims, a people who once have tafted the bleffings of liberty will dare to oppofe, will rife to refift, and eventually will obtain. It was the exceffive tyranny of the Conqueror and his fucceffors that called forth the latent oppreffed fpirit of Englifhmen, the feeds of liberty they had planted—The vegetation may be checked, may to a defpot's flattered eye be eradicated, but the Sun of Britifh freedom has ever difpelled the cloud of defpotifm, re-animated the hereditary feeds, and the vegetation has made arbitrary Monarchs tremble.

The formidable power of the firft Norman Princes, who could crufh the moft powerful Baron at their pleafure, excited a fpirit of union to deliberate among the different ranks of people, and clofe confederacies took place, to concert a refiftance againft the enormous power of the Crown. Here the Barons, as the chief landholders, affociated,

ciated, and freely expatiated on the tyranny of the judicial proceedings, and the slavish injunctions of the foreft laws *, the feverity of which was particularly oppreffive. In thefe confederacies a difcuffion of the precife terms and meaning of the new laws impofed by the Conqueror, muft have appeared unintelligible to a great majority, the interpretation of them by the Barons could not have been conveyed to the capacities of the lower orders, without a colourable ray of fophiftry, which would naturally excite an enquiry into the focial rights of men, and renew to their minds the free principles of the Saxon inftitutions. The confequence followed, if we judge from effects, of their thorough conviction, that a limited power exceeded is a power forfeited; that equality of privileges is the firft principle of fociety; that the union of power and property, in the hands of one or of a few, operates againft the common intereft of a community and againft focial right, and its oppreffive laws or right of action may be oppofed by a fimilar right.

* Another violent alteration of the Englifh Conftitution (in confequence of the Invafion) confifted in the depopulation of whole countries for the purpofe of the King's royal diverfion, and fubjecting both them and all the ancient forefts of the kingdom to the unreasonable feverities of foreft laws imported from the Continent, whereby the flaughter of a beaft was made almoft as penal as the death of a man. In the Saxon times, though no man was allowed to kill or chace the King's deer, yet he might ftart any game, purfue and kill it on his own eftate. *Black. Comm. vol. IV. p.* 415.

Hence

Hence by an eafy affimilation of principles, the fubordinate claffes became infpired with the true fpirit of liberty, and we find them in the fubfequent reign of Henry III. ftipulating for the fame conditions as the Barons themfelves; and the Barons by * uniting with, and confirming the people in their rights, in order to oppofe the rapacity of the Roman Church, and the power of the Crown, created that fpirit of dignified human nature in John Bull, which having now afcertained the juft prerogatives of the Crown, will ever check the overbearing fpirit of an Ariftocracy, and preferve the Conftitution from arbitrary power, and the no lefs dangerous State, a convulfed Republic.

Some adventitious circumftances concurred to produce thefe rifing fparks of ancient liberty. After the death of William Rufus, Henry I. fecured his fucceffion to the throne, to the exclufion of his elder brother Robert, by promifing to reftore the laws of Edward the Confeffor, and other confirmations of Saxon liberties, which fecured the people in their perfons and property; for this purpofe he granted a charter, which in the reign of King John the Barons made the foundation of *Magna Charta.* By the irregular fucceffions of Henry I. and Stephen, the people made fome advances for the regaining of political liberty; and

* Hume, Appendix, No. II. p. 113.

the

the conceffions firft made by Henry were particularly demanded at the coronation of every fubfequent Monarch; but by them they had been confidered merely as appendages to the Crown, to be
put on or off at pleafure. John at his coronation
took the ufual oaths, but foon after difcovered his
defpotic nature, by the horrid murder of his ne-
phew Arthur. Imbruing his hands in the blood
of fo near a relation, fhocked the humanity, and
roufed the indignation of the whole kingdom. On
his arrival in England from the French provinces,
he exerted the Royal prerogatives and the foreft
laws to that degree of exceffive feverity, that the
dormant fpirit of confederated liberty now openly
manifefted itfelf throughout the nation. The caufe
of freedom became the caufe of juftice; the caufe
of equal privileges the caufe of truth; the union
of the people was fober refiftance; the efforts of
the Barons were dignified; the oppofition glorious
and laudable. Hence were obtained the Great
Charter of Liberties, which involves all the chief
outlines of a legal Government, and provides for
the equal diftribution of juftice, and free enjoyment of property, which Mr. Hume emphatically
terms * *the great objects for which political fociety was
at firft founded by men; which the people have a perpetual and unalienable right to recall, and which no
time nor precedent, nor ftatute, nor pofitive inftitution,*

* Hift. Eng. Vol. II. p. 88.

ought

ought to deter them from keeping ever uppermoſt in their thoughts and attention.

By this famous Charter, the Saxon free principles were incorporated with the feudal ſyſtem, which laid the foundation of our truly limited Monarchy; and whoever at the preſent period reflects on the incorporation of thoſe two oppoſite principles, and the preſent connexions and ſubordinations of our elaborate Conſtitution, cannot ſufficiently admire the limitations and prerogatives of the Chief Magiſtrate. With the feudal ſyſtem introduced by William I. many valuable energies were obtained; and this ſyſtem, however at firſt ſubverſive of the common rights of the people, has through ſucceſſive ages been open to improvement, and as knowledge became progreſſively more general, it has been in a continual habit of acquiring perfection. At the Revolution it was pruned of its chief exceſſes, and attempted to be modelled to the intereſt of all. But practice ever tending to make theory bluſh, it remains for the preſent age to temper the energy of the Norman ſyſtem with the lax principles of the old Engliſh, by a Parliamentary Reform; this will produce that neceſſary equilibrium, or balance of property and power, which is the baſis of a limited Monarchy; and the firſt principle of our Conſtitution.

H   SECT.

SECTION V.

Remarks on Political Liberty, from the Confirmation of Magna Charta, under King John, to the Succession of the House of Stuart.

THROUGHOUT the Englifh Hiftory, we muft carry in our minds the facred truth, that political liberty is the birth-right of Britons; and though the feveral articles in Magna Charta, through the refinements made by the chicanery of modern law, are now confidered as bare of circumftances, and too concife, and the charter itfelf an ufelefs fcroll, yet it contains, among other articles of univerfal juftice and equal right, an explicit confirmation of the right of political liberty. This important article * is as follows :—" That if the " King, or his Juftices, or Bailiffs, or any of his " Minifters, offend any perfon contrary to any of " the faid articles, or tranfgrefs any article of this " peace and fecurity, and that fuch mifcarriage be " made known to four of the faid five and twenty " Barons, thofe four Barons fhall go to the King, " or to his Jufticiary, if the King be out of the " realm, declaring to him that fuch an abufe is " committed, and fhall defire him to caufe it fpee- " dily to be redreffed; and if the King, or (if he be

* 64th.

" out.

" out of the realm) his Jufticiary do not redrefs it;
" Then the faid four Barons fhall report the fame to
" the refidue of the faid five and twenty Barons; and
" then thofe five and twenty Barons, with the Com-
" monalty of England, may diftrefs us by all the ways
" they can; to wit, by feizing on our caftles, lands
" and poffeffions; and by what other means they can,
" till it be amended, as they fhall adjudge, faving
" our own perfon, the perfon of our Queen, and the
" perfons of our children; and when it is amended,
" they fhall be fubject to us as before."

The language of this Covenant is very harfh, and the condition itfelf appears ill fuited to pro- duce either peace or good order in the State, or to affure the real liberty of the fubject. It was no doubt fuitable to the genius of the times; civil liberty could not thrive in a community altogether military, and in a ftate of vaffalage; but with the abolition of this military dependance, the Confti- tution became better known; and though the fub- ftance of this article has been modelled to the exi- gencies of good government, the people have not, nor cannot relinquifh the principle, it being their indefeafible, unalienable right. By this condition it muft have followed, that the power of the King was very materially retrenched, and it muft have thrown an immenfe power into the hands of the Ariftocracy; the truth of which appears, with fome trifling intermiffion, down to the Revolution. The

H 2

whole

whole of this long period feems to have been a fluctuating ftruggle between political liberty and the ufurpations of Monarchs, Priefts and ambitious Barons. Upon this exprefs ftipulation in Magna Charta, on behalf of the commonalty, to refift the higher powers, the memorable oppofitions of Tyler, Cade, &c. were lawfully made. Recurrences to political liberty which muft render their conduct venerable in the eftimation of every impartial and fincere friend to the Conftitution, which appears to owe its excellence to extreme cafes and extreme arguments. The true fpirit of liberty boldly faces its enemies; confcious truth gives ardour to common right; and though tyranny prevail, and prieftcraft triumph, we are bound by reafon and hiftory to acknowledge that the trueft friends to mankind have been thofe who have nobly facrificed their private interefts for the public good, and glorioufly bled in the common caufe.

As this famous Charter is the firft on record of the *Leges Scriptæ*, or Statute Laws, and lays the foundation of our prefent form of Parliament, the controverfies which have arifen on the origin of the Houfe of Commons, and the rights of the people to an equal reprefentation, are reduced to mere quibbles about words. If we take an enlarged view of thofe circumftances which attend all revolutions, our prejudices will not then afcribe Magna Charta and the being of Parliament to the grace and

and favour of Monarchs; nor can the moft enthu-
fiaftic advocate for liberty wholly afcribe them to
the forefight and wifdom of their anceftors. It has
been found in every material innovation or change
of Government, that lefs is due to the fagacity of
the laity or the virtues of the clergy, than to thofe
fortuitous events which conftitute the laws of the
univerfe; to thofe immutable laws, which ever
operating on matter, produce thofe feeming irre-
gularities in human fyftems, which render every
inftitution mutable, and every Government a type
of the human heart. With this remark we fhall
confider the circumftances of this important period, and we fhall find the obtaining Magna
Charta, as well as the fubfequent revolutions, was
owing to the fluctuating principles of property.

The feudal fyftem introduced by the Conqueror
threw the balance of property, and with that the
balance of power, entirely into the hands of the
Crown, which created * a fubordination of vaffalage from the King to the meaneft gentleman, and
the confequent flavery of the lower people. The
King being the fupreme Lord of all the landed
property, it followed that † all the lands in England were derived from, and holden, mediately or
immediately from the Crown; and which William

---

* Hume, vol. II. p. 265.   † Black. Comm. vol. IV. p. 418.

had

had conferred on his chief Barons, fubject to the
military fervices of 60,000 Knights fees.

But the balance of property, having its foundation
in nature, cannot be immutably fixed by either of
the two extremes, a Norman feudal tenure, or an
Utopian levelling fyftem. The ufurped power of a
few in a large community cannot retain it for any
length of time from the many, particularly when the
public mind is impreffed with the fpirit of liberty,
or the diffufion of knowledge has undermined fuperftition, and difpelled the cloud of ignorance,
which two enemies of reafon and truth are the
main fprings on which defpotifm and prieftcraft
move. The Houfe of Commons therefore, and
the partial reprefentation of the people, originated
from the variable principles of the balance of property, by the accidental divifions of the exorbitant eftates of the Norman Barons, and the confequent abolition of military tenures, * thefe immenfe
Baronies were divided by provifions to younger
children, by partitions to co-heirs, by fale, or by
efcheating to the King, who gratified a great number of his courtiers by dealing them out in fmaller
portions, by which a middle rank was formed,
which became very numerous, and at the period
of obtaining Magna Charta formed a very refpect-

* Hume, Vol. II. p. 268.

able

able order in the State ; and as they were all immediate vaffals of the Crown by military tenure, they
were, by the principles of the feudal law, entitled
to a feat in the national councils. It is unreafon-
able to fuppofe, that when the various divifions and
fub-divifions of property had abolifhed the military
tenures, which entitled the tenants to a feat in the
national councils, they fhould have forfeited their
right to a future fhare in the motions of Government, or have entirely difregarded that privilege.
On the contrary, it is more reafonable to conclude,
they became more anxious for their property, and
attentive to their rights. By the abolition of military tenures, perfonal fervices were exchanged for
pecuniary fupplies ; the minds of men were turned
to agriculture and commerce ; property acquired
an eftimation, and became the firft moving principle in private life, as well as the great object of
the public mind ; this great period may therefore
be regarded as the dawn of a revolution from a
military to a commercial age ; the obtaining Magna
Charta laid the foundation of that great event ;
the Reformation gave it fpirit and motion ; and
under Elizabeth it affumed a body and figure.

The accidental and gradual abolition of military
tenures accelerated the attainment of that due balance of property which is the foundation of a free
Government, by conftituting a Legiflative power,
partly compofed of the labouring part of the com-.

H 4   munity,

munity, to counteract the oppreffion and encroach-
ments of the rich and powerful. This revival of the
ancient Britifh free principles arofe, as before obferved, by the union of the Barons with the fubordinate ranks, to concert refiftance againft the
Crown. And the future right to this co-operation
was confirmed by the 64th article of the Charter,
which impowers the commonalty of England to
oppofe the King if he violated their liberties. The
fubfequent civil wars to which this condition gave
birth, prove how little civil Government was
known in that military age; a rifing of the commonalty in England in arms againft the King was
productive of infinite evils, and attended with ani-
mofities for which death itfelf could only atone.
But happily, the immortal Earl of Leicefter laid
the foundation of an inftitution, * which in procefs
of time became one of the moft ufeful and powerful
members of the national Conftitution. This great
Baron, under Henry III. glorioufly oppofing the
thunders of the Roman Church, and the weaknefs
and wickednefs of the King, fummoned a Parliament in the year 1265, to which he ordered returns to be made of two Knights from each fhire,
and Deputies from the cities and boroughs. Upon
this firft precedent of our prefent Houfe of Commons, it is impoffible to fplit and divide an idea,
and render a general covenant a partial one. If

* Hume, vol. II. p. 211.

the

Commonalty of England were impowered by
Magna Charta to oppofe the abufe of their liberties
by the King, the commonalty of all England are
entitled, without a fhadow of doubt, to an equal
reprefentation in the Houfe of Commons, the origin of which arofe from changing a hoftile refiftance into a legal form. This is the true principle
on which the Houfe of Commons is founded. It
is general, it is univerfal, it is the birth-right of
Britons; that this principle; which extends to all,
and is the right of every man, fhould be reduced
to common right in abftract, to partial reprefentation and monopoly, could only arife from the ftate
of military. vaffalage under which the great majority
of the people laboured for many years, added to the
ignorance and fuperftition which for many fubfequent centuries the Roman Church encouraged.

In the fubfequent reign of Edward I. this precedent of Leicefter's, which was in fact * a privilege. covenanted in Magna Charta, obtained fo
much on the public mind, that Edward found his
edicts for raifing talliages and aids could not be
carried into effect, without fummoning reprefentatives from cities and boroughs to Parliament; and
one of the Parliaments of this reign obtained from
Edward the moft important ftatute in the whole
Englifh code. The ftatute *de tallagio non conce-*

* Blackftone Comm. vol. IV. p. 225.

dendo

dendo, which decrees that no tax fhall be laid, nor impoft levied, without the joint confent of the Lords and the Commons.¹ * This ftatute was the engine which protected the Charter itfelf, and by the help of which the people were thenceforth to make a legal conqueft over the Crown.

Many arbitrary writers, I conclude, embrace a miftake, merely to accommodate their principles, when they affirm that the reprefentatives of the people returned from cities and borough towns were an order of men who had ever been confidered as too mean to enjoy a place in the national councils. This conclufion would not have been doubted, if we were not informed, that, under the feudal law, military tenants were entitled to a feat in the Norman Parliaments, and that the Houfe of Commons in its prefent form derives its origin from the abolition of military tenures, and from the covenant in Magna Charta impowering the Barons and the commonalty of England to oppofe the oppreffion of the Monarch. Hence the term Commons, from the word commonalty, was merely giving a new name to the fame order of men. The military tenants were the Knights and Gentry, who upon this revolution got themfelves elected for their refpective counties, cities, and boroughs, in which they refided; and with the progrefs of com-

* De Lolme, c. 11. p. 40.

merce

merce and literature, obtained a preponderance in the Conſtitution, and a powerful influence in the motions of Government, a conſequence which naturally followed, after ſhaking off the burden of military vaſſalage. The repreſentatives of the people elected in the cities, counties, and boroughs, were from this period legally eſtabliſhed as a conſtituent part of the Conſtitution; and it was ordained under Edward III.*, that Parliaments ſhall be held once a year, or oftener if need be, which was a † renewal of the Saxon law of holding Parliaments.

And a Houſe of Commons as thus conſtituted, when freely choſen and freely acting, has, in numerous inſtances, proved the only aſſurance for the free operation of the Conſtitution, and the ſtable ſupport of freedom. And notwithſtanding it was by variable, yet progreſſive acceſſions, that it became a permanent and powerful eſtabliſhment, at that period it was a very important point obtained for the body of people, to convene in a legal manner, armed with liberty, reaſon, and truth, inſtead of the ſhield, the buckler, and battering ram, to demoliſh the King's caſtle, and ſeize on his poſſeſſions for redreſs of grievances.

* 4 Edw. III. c. 14. and 36 Edw. III. c. 9.
† Mirror of Juſtice, c. 1. ſ. 3. and c. 5. ſ. 1.

In

In the subfequent reign of Edward II. the Commons * began to annex petitions to the bills by which they granted subfidies. This was the firft dawn of their legiflative authority. Under Edward III. they declared they would not in future acknowledge any law to which they had not exprefsly affented. Soon after this they exerted a privilege, in which confifted, at this time, one of the great bulwarks of the Conftitution; they impeached, and procured to be condemned, fome of the Minifters of State. Under the weak and turbulent reign of Richard II. the King endeavoured to poifon the integrity, and oppofe the growing independence of the Commons, by fecret and corrupt influence. One article alledged againft him, and to which he confeffed, was in the following words, as they appear on the Rolls—† 19 *Item.*

" Although by ftatute, and the cuftom of his
" realm, in the calling of every Parliament, and
" to lay open their grievances, and to profecute
" for remedies thereupon as they think fit, not-
" withftanding the faid King, that in his Parlia-
" ments he might obtain his will, which was rafh,
" often directed his mandates to his Sheriffs, that
" they fhould return certain perfons, nominated by
" the King himfelf, as Knights of the Shires,
" which Knights indeed he could make pliable to
" him, and as he very often did, fometimes by

* De Lolme, c. iii. p. 41.　　† Henry IV. m. 20.

" various

" various threats and terrors, and fometimes by
" gifts, to confent to thofe things which were
" prejudicial to the realm, and extremely burden-
" fome to the people."

From this reign down to that of Henry VII.
was a continued fcene of infurrections and wars.
No part of the Englifh hiftory fince the Conqueft
is fo uncertain, and fo little authentic, as the wars
of the Houfes of York and Lancafter; at the conclufion of which the nobility were brought to a
humble fubmiffion to the ftern prerogatives of the
Crown. The people were reduced to their former
ftate of vaffalage, and the improvement of the Conftitution wholly neglected—*Nam filent leges inter
arma*—and we are left to deplore a difgraceful period of hiftory, * a fcene of horror, bloodfhed,
favage manners, arbitrary executions, and treacherous, difhonourable conduct in all parties.

The union of thefe two contending families by
the marriage of Henry VII. quelled each jarring
intereft; and the reformation in the next reign,
which occafioned a great revolution in manners
and property, paved the way for afcertaining the
equilibrium neceffary in the Three Eftates, by im-
perceptibly weakening the Ariftocracy, advancing
the Commons, and limiting the Prerogative; and

* Hume, vol. III. p. 3}.

finally

finally concurred to the reftoration of the ancient limited Monarchy, which was confirmed by the Revolution. Yet in the intermediate reigns, the Crown, while this great Revolution was maturing, became progreffively * more arbitrary, by thofe very means which afterwards reduced its power.

The wars of the two Rofes put an entire ftop to trade for feveral years; and the Commons were reduced to fuch an abject dependance on the King, the Clergy, and the Barons, during the defpotic reign of Henry. VIII. that they feemed to have totally loft that infpiration for their ancient liberties, which pervaded and animated the whole State during the reigns of John, Henry, and Edward I. And no reign in the Englifh hiftory holds out a more ferious truth than this of Henry VIII. For though there be no danger that the nation, while animated with the fpirit of liberty, will again relapfe into fuch a bafe and fervile dependance on a rude tyrannic barbarian, yet the principle teaches the important leffon, That Government, in the hands of an ambitious Prince, may be modelled to the defpotic bias of his heart, though the forms of a free Conftitution remain; and that thofe barriers which political liberty has provided in the Confti-tution to maintain freedom, life, and property, may be made, by direct or indirect means, falvos.

* Black. Comm. vol. IV. p. 433.

for

for the grosseft enormities. Henry extorted loans from the people which he never meant to repay, and loaded them with oppreffive taxes; and the firft men in the nation were made to tremble at his difpleafure, againft whom he perpetrated violences the moft enormous. But he never attempted to abolifh the Parliament, or even to retrench its doubtful privileges. On the contrary, he made it the prime minifter of his tyranny, the paffive inftrument of his outrages againft liberty life, and law. It fanctioned his defpotic and fanguinary meafures, and authorized his oppreffive taxes; and to the eternal difgrace of the Parliaments of this reign, they enacted that the King's Proclamations fhould have the force of law, and by creating a long lift of chimerical treafons, have rendered the memory of them infamous.

From thefe facts we may conclude, that the long civil wars of the Rofes had fo depreffed the national fpirit, that as the vigour of the national body failed by the divifion of its parts, the fovereign power of the Crown became by confequence more arbitrary and unlimited; and England at this æra was arrived at an ebb, which was either to flow to flavery or freedom. At the moment when tranfitory evils had thrown the Conftitution into the gulph of Defpotifm, the Reformation by a fortuitous event, wafted the bark of Freedom over the quickfands of Prieftcraft and Tyranny, roufed the

Genius

Genius of Liberty, which in the fubfequent reigns animated the fpirit of the nation to affert the privi- leges of a free people; and happily that facred fpirit of liberty has never fince forfaken the Britifh ifle.

In the fubfequent reign of Edward VI. the tyrannical laws and new-fangled treafons inftituted by Henry, his father, were happily abolifhed. This virtuous youth was adorned with the light of reafon, with a heart graced with promifing difpofi- tions, and a capacity to learn and judge; but to the infinite concern of the friends of liberty and the Proteftant caufe, his reign was cut fhort under his people's fmiles; and fo eafy is the tranfition from human joy to forrow, by the blood-thirft Mary, their fmiles were fucceeded by tears. Milton's Satan under Papal colours ravaged the land, revelled in the tortures of reafon and truth; and in this *mon- ftrous* reign, ignorance was no protection, when even brutes were facrificed to the Popifh faith. On the acceffion of Elizabeth, England, reviving from the general ftupor, began to breathe; and Elizabeth embracing the Proteftant religion, blef- fed the Ifle with a long and brilliant reign. But fuch was the analogy between fovereign power and defpotifm, that a Princefs the moft enlightened, and of the moft fplendid talents, could not fepa- rate the long cherifhed idea of former reigns from that which is a Sovereign's ultimate happinefs and final fecurity—*the affections of their people.* The

Star

Star Chamber was ſtill continued, and the High Commiſſion Court even inſtituted to ſyſtemize confidence and enforce obedience. The extreme miſeries of the laſt reign, and the glory of this leſſened the tyranny of theſe inſtitutions; and the wiſdom of Elizabeth, as it tempered oppreſſion, the people in the admiration of the one, overlooked the other.

SECTION

SECTION VI.

Remarks on Political Liberty, from the Succession of the House of Stuart to the Revolution.

THE nation at this period began to find the happy effects of the Reformation. The great alteration in property advanced the power of the Commons; the art of printing began to disseminate learning throughout the State, and to enlarge the minds of men; trade and navigation were suddenly carried on to an amazing extent; an inundation of wealth flowed in upon the merchants and middling ranks; the Popish Clergy had been detected in their frauds and abuses, and stripped of their lands and revenues, were left trembling for their very existence. " * But there " is no abuse so great in civil society, as not to " be attended with beneficial consequences to " some : and in the beginning of reformations, " the loss of these advantages is always felt very " sensibly, while the benefits resulting from the " change is the slow effect of time." This accounts for the prejudices of the House of Stuart in favour of Popery, that engine of despotism, which was

* Hume, vol. III. p. 236.

the caufe of the civil wars, and the unfortunate ca-
taftrophe of that high prerogative family. That
Monarchs fhould favour every inftitution which
deprives the people of their rights and liberties, is
the natural confequence of human ambition. But
that there fhould be found any confiderable difinterefted number, or even one individual, poffeffed
of this aftonifhing predilection for defpotifm, is
wonderful. The partifans of that unhappy family,
and the advocates of the prefent day for arbitrary
power, evince how difficult it is to eradicate prejudices when deeply rooted in the human breaft.
The partifans of the Stuarts may be compared to
· Mary I. who declared *, " She never read Pro-
" teftant books, and thanked God that as fhe
" never had, fo fhe hoped never to read any of
" them." Ignorance in an illiterate age may be
admitted as a veil for many enormities, but the
enemies to liberty and reform among the moderns
can only plead felf-intereft—Individual integrity,
the public good, and the national freedom, they
confider as meritorious facrifices for their own aggrandizement. Hence ignorance, felf-intereft,
and prejudice, eclipfe the hiftory of man. One
age decries the ignorance and prejudices of the
laft; fucceeding ages the corruption and vices of
the times; and pofterity, finally, refts on the
frailty of human nature.

* Hume, vol. IV. p. 436.

Of

Of all the frailties in the human catalogue, prejudice is the leaft defenfible; it deprives the mind
of its nobleft faculty, that reafoning principle
which diftinguifhes a human being from a
brute; and though ignorance be the caufe, yet
it fcorns the conviction of the fact by which it
is flattered. With this ignoble principle the Stuart
family afcended the Britifh Throne. Ignorant of
civil government, though learned in the law of defpotic precedents; and prejudiced by the example
of their predeceffors, their narrow minds could not
perceive the amazing revolution both of property
and religious fentiment which had taken place
fince the Reformation.

James, the firft King of the Stuart race, was lefs
a tyrant than an enthufiaft. Enthufiafm delights
in chimera; and in the brain of James it alighted
on a fruitful foil. The divinity of Kings was his
political creed; the abfurd doctrine of divine
right had feized on his mind, and his tongue
chimed with the theme. With the pedantry of a
collegian, in his private converfation, his writings, and his public fpeeches, he was continually
afferting *, That the authority of Kings was not
to be controlled any more than that of God himfelf; like him they were omnipotent; and that
the privileges which the people laid claim to as

* See his fpeeches made in Parliament in the year 1610—21.

their

their inheritance and birth-right were no more
than the effects of the grace and toleration of his
Royal anceſtors. Thus James oſtentatiouſly diſ-
played thoſe fallacies which his anceſtors and the
Pope had invented. Paſſive obedience and non-
reſiſtance had been taught by the Clergy; but
former Monarchs were content in the enjoyment
of that deception which James had the impru-
dence to publiſh. The liberty of the preſs, then,
in its dawn, contributed, notwithſtanding the
Star-Chamber, to diſſeminate ſuch ſalutary notions among all orders of the people, as detected
the ſophiſms delivered from the throne and the
pulpit, and finally concurred in the refutation of
the divinity of Kings, by teaching Charles I. his
ſon, that Kings rule by the grace of the people,
and that they never can aſſume the ſacred privilege of ruling by the grace of God, but when they
govern according to the laws of the land, according to general liberty, virtue, and juſtice.

The private character of Charles is repreſented as
virtuous, but his public character vicious; Nature
had been kind, but his education, as in the words
of the Poet, triumphed.

> By education moſt men are miſled,
> So we believe becauſe we were ſo bred;
> The prieſt continues what the nurſe began,
> And thus the child impoſes on the man.

Encircled

Encircled by a few, who in their hearts cherilhed the doctrine of the Pope, yet wore the femblance of the Proteftant Church, Charles was inceffantly flattered with his father's maxim of Divine right, and the unlimited prerogative of his predeceffors, which he manifefted on all occafions. The nation detected the fiction, and in turn freely canvaffed the prerogatives of the Crown. The fcrutiny proved fatal; rather let us fay, when reafon and juftice prevail over arbitrary power and prieftcraft, *a triumph*. Political liberty was afferted and maintained by the reprefentatives of the people; the Commons alone ftood firm, when the power of the Nobles was vanquifhed.

Among the Commons were men of profeffed abilities, and acknowledged Statefmen—Men who entered warmly into conftitutional meafures—. Men whofe views were as folid as their principles were juft; thefe oppofed to the *jure divino* of Charles the *vox populi vox Dei*—The Divinity of law—in the law alone was the Divine Power; and every law founded on liberty and juftice had a claim for obedience, Royalty itfelf not exempt. This was the voice of the people fanctioned by the immutable laws of the Deity. But the King had been taught, that the fupreme power was inherent in the Crown; that the legiflative authority muft comport with the dictates of his heart,

that

that the executive authority could only originate from the active impulse of his divine mind.

Both powers thus claimed a divine origin; but it requires not the fagacity of a Pope to perceive, that the people's was that of the Gofpel, the King's that of the Alcoran. Charles became a convert, but by his apoftacy met his fate. The ftern brow of Prerogative, fupported by the delufion of Divine right, could not brook the fancied ignominy of relaxing its fovereign power, by fubmitting to the future wifdom and control of Parliament. Charles repeatedly diffolved his Parliaments for their integrity and patriotifm, and continued to practife every illegal meafure. The perverfion of the law by corrupt judges, and the imprifonment of the fubject for default of payment of fhip-money, and other obnoxious and arbitrary taxes, operated in fanning the flame of difcord among all ranks of people, and created thofe lafting prejujudices, which his conceffions in his laft Parliament could not allay.

The famous Petition of Right, framed by a Committee of his third Parliament, fets forth, in an explicit manner the violent abufes of the prerogative, and beft explains the pretenfions of the Commons, who appear to have affumed no unprecedented privileges, or demanded unufual powers. The Bill of Rights, which was enacted in confe-

quence,

quence, was declaratory of the known ſtatutes of
the land, and a recognition of the Great Charter,
and that important ſtatute of Edward I. for raiſing
taillages, which is the bulwark of the Conſtitution.

The firmneſs and independence of the Parliaments of this reign afford the higheſt example
of their ſpecific utility. The conſequences which
followed amply ſhew the abſolute neceſſity that
the repreſentatives of the people ſhould be independent of the frowns or ſecret influence of the
Crown, but that they ſhould never be independent
of the choice of the people. Free Parliaments and
frequent elections are the deputies of political liberty, and the members and ſpirit of the Conſtitution, and cannot be annulled without annihilating the machine. When Parliaments are free, civil liberty is aſſured from every act, overt or ſecret, that tyranny can invent, or proud ambition
ſtimulate.

Happy had Charles been, happy indeed would
have been the nation, had he as ſolicitouſly endeavoured to gain the affections of his people as he
was induſtrious in every chicanery to trample on
their ſacred rights, and violate every principle of
juſtice. But the King could not reconcile re-
ſtraints or limitations of that Divine power with
which the Great Author of Nature had veſted him;
an authority, which for baſe mortals to diſpute, in
his

his eftimation, amounted to blafphemy. His eva-
fions in confirming the Bill of Rights prove his
fubmiffion was concealed hypocrify ; his conduct
and difcourfe dfcovered the infincerity of his heart.
The firft opportunity that offered he violated all
that he had done, diffolved the Parliament, and
in future was determined to govern by himfelf fupreme, which he did for eleven years, when his
various defpotic ways and means failing, his ur-
gent neceffities induced him to call another Parliament, which poffeffing the fame patriotic fpirit
of thofe which had formerly been the occafion of
his difpleafure, he abruptly diffolved it, but foon
after convoked another, which wifely began its
career by impeaching, and procuring to be pu-
nifhed the King's evil counfellors, the fecret enemies of liberty, peace, and concord ; and the
mutual agreement of the King and Commons bid
fair to reftore once more the calm return of pro-
mifed harmony, Charles having in Parliament
abolifhed the Star Chamber and High Commiffion
Courts, and enacted ftatutes for Triennial Parliaments, for afcertaining the foreft laws, and renouncing Ship Money and other exactions. But
the true caufe of the national difcontent under the
Stuart family now manifefted itfelf. The cruelties
of Mary had left an indelible ftain on the Catholic
faith, and created a jealoufy in the Britifh breaft,
which the leaft breath of fufpicion fanned into a
flame. Unfortunately this family indirectly coun-

tenanced

tenanced the Roman church : and in the dawn of
general literature, it followed, that theological
points, difcuffed by ruftic reafon, would beget fa-
naticifm. Unacquainted with logical refinements
and the fubtleties of fchoolmen, any learned oppofition to their opinions they confidered as fophiftry; their minds dwelt on enthufiafm as infpiration : and in a common caufe, which under the gofpel difpenfation, required the laws to be adminiftered with juftice and mercy, and equal right to be
done, where each had an equal claim to the enjoyment of liberty, it was a natural confequence
that the Puritans fhould imagine they poffeffed the
Divine favour, and that their caufe was that of the
Lord's. The extremes which followed were in
proportion to the oppreffion fuffered. Religious
diffenfions were now rifing to a flame. The King
had broke with the Scots, and the Irifh were in
rebellion; and Charles having, by his former conduct, loft the confidence of the nation, his fituation became defperate. The Commons, to fecure
their authority, had taken advantage of the King's
neceffities, and obtained from him the fatal confent for their unlimited duration, exempt from the
control of his prerogative; which rafh meafure
was attended with the moft fatal confequences.
One tyrant is more tolerable than five hundred;
the one has his moments of relaxation, the many
are invariably and inflexibly the fame; the gather-
ing ftorm now raged from every quarter; the moft
discordant

difcordant paffions which harrafs the human mind, compofed the element of anarchy; and in the thunder ftorm of civil war, the unhappy Charles fell, an awful example of lawlefs majefty; and the Commonwealth which fucceeded is another lawlefs example, and fhews too evidently the wide difference between theoretical models of polity and practical ones. On this overthrow of the Conftitution, Mr. De Lolme judicioufly obferves, the " Englifh made fruitlefs attempts to fubftitute a " Republican Government in its ftead, fubjected " at firft to the power of the principal leaders in " the Long Parliament; they faw it afterwards " parcelled out among the Chiefs of different bo- " dies of troops, and thus fhifting without end " from one kind of fubjection to another; they " were at length convinced, that an attempt to " eftablifh liberty in a great nation, by making " the people interfere in the common bufinefs of " Government, is of all attempts the moft chi- " merical; that the authority of ALL, with which " men are amufed, is in reality no more than the " authority of a few powerful individuals who di- " vide the Republic. They at laft refted in the " bofom of the only Conftitution which is fit for " a great State and a free people. I mean that " in which a chofen number deliberate, and a " fingle hand executes."

How

How neceffary is Monarchy when duly limited? How futile and vain are the attempts of a multitude to maintain liberty on a pure foundation, when there is no object to obey, but a code of laws executed by a number of men, equal in perfon, equal in claim, and equal in right? Where they demand allegiance they create jealoufy; where they enforce fubjection, they fow envy and malice; a divifion of intereft takes place; the rich and powerful maintain an ufurped authority; and the people, after a momentary excefs of liberty, find, to their forrow, the vain delufion of natural right, the chimerical dream of unreftrained liberty. An arbitrary Government, by reftraining the paffions, and enforcing fubjection, is in fact far the more eligible and happy than a convulfed Republic.

From this memorable ftruggle for the prerogatives of the Crown and the privileges of Parliament, there arifes two reflections. 1ft. That whether the Executive Power, by coercive meafures can fubdue the Parliament to its will, or by fecretly and corruptly influencing the reprefentatives of the people, can feparate the common intereft, the Government becomes arbitrary and abfolute. 2nd. That when the reprefentatives of the people can render themfelves a permanent body, by an overt act obtained by confent of the King for their unlimited duration, or when a Parliament

liament fhall abolifh the kingly office, or when
Members of Parliament, by obtaining boroughs,
can make their election independent of their conftituents, the Government likewife becomes arbitrary and abfolute.

The conclufion from thefe facts and reafonings
is the confirmation of that known apothegm, That
England never can be ruined but by a Parliament. The fecret and corrupt influence of the
Executive Power over the Parliaments of the prefent century, afford a degrading contraft to the
Commons of Charles's reign. Pofterity will not
again experience overt refponfible acts from the
Crown. Its very antagonifts are now become the
inftruments of its power, and oppreffion has fhifted
fides. This evil can only be remedied by an equal
and free reprefentation, and the public mind is
preparing for the event.

Charles II. was wholly indebted to the deftruction of civil liberty by the Commonwealth for his
reftoration. By a well-timed and judicious exercife of political liberty by a convention of the
States, the Conftitution was regained; but it was
found that the King had not profited by the example of his father, the fame arbitrary principles
mantling in his veins, operated in a converfe direction, more plaufible, but not the lefs dangerous.
Charles, by the diverfity of his fortune, had formed
a judgment

a judgment of men, which a thorough knowledge of the world confirms, That a principle of self-interest predominates in general to the exclusion of public virtue, and too often that of moral obligations. He saw the error of his father in contending with a Parliament, and with a people who inherited a Constitution formed by laws breathing a bold and independent spirit of liberty. The last House of Commons that consented to a law for its own unlimited duration, which had abolished the elective power of the people for near twenty years, furnished him with a precedent, that the representatives of the people were willing to make a separate interest from their constituents, and that by a Parliament the outward form and figure of the Constitution might be preserved, yet he might by indirect means extend his prerogative to any height he chose; for if he could separate the interest of the Commons from that of the people, by influencing a majority to the interests of the Crown, he could govern the nation at his will, leaving the people destitute of any power to redress their grievances. Upon this principle, after the convention of the States had settled him on the throne, he issued his writs for convoking a Parliament; and the people, long harrassed by the anarchy of the Commonwealth, submitted the election to his own management, by which means he procured the memorable pensioned Parliament, and afterwards was guilty of every dissipation and tyranny,

uniting

uniting with the high prerogative of his father the principles of a debauchee ; and the national fpirit, depreffed with continued fcenes of defpotifm, tamely fuffered her moft virtuous patriots to be inhumanly butchered. But notwithftanding the tyrannical difpofition of the King *, the happy concurrence of circumftances was fuch, that from this reign we may date not only the re-eftablifhment of our Church and Monarchy, but alfo the complete reftitution of Englifh liberty, for the firft time fince its total abolition at the Conqueft, by abolifhing the flavifh tenures of the feudal fyftem, which removed thofe oppreffive appendages which incumbered the eftates of the fubject, as alfo providing additional fecurity of his perfon from imprifonment, by that great bulwark of the Conftitution, the Habeas Corpus Act, by conftituting triennial Parliaments, the Teft and Corporation Acts, and other wholefome ftatutes, which added fuch weight to the Commons, as gave them fufficient power and influence effectually to refift the invafions of the Royal prerogative, which the next reign fully exemplified.

James II. inherited the family fpirit of Divine right, and by his Popifh partifans improved on the principles of his brother, by laying the axe at once to the root of freedom. But in attempting

* Black. Comm. vol. IV. p. 438.

to render the Government as abfolute as the In-
quifition of their fofter parent at Rome, roufed
John Bull's anceftors to exert the privileges of a
free people, and by the Revolution excluded this
Catholic race for ever.

We are now arrived at that grand epoch in
which political liberty was exercifed in a moft
confpicuous and orderly manner, highly to the
interefts of the nation, and honourable to the
acting parties. Political liberty ever infpires the
moft liberal views; upon this principle I fhall
continue my remarks on this important period.

With the progrefs of the Englifh Hiftory, we
are told the Conftitution became better underftood
and improved. Upon this theorem, the relation
between Governors and the governed, and the nature of a limited monarchy, acquires at the prefent day arguments drawn from the experienced
effects of the Revolution; and though, perhaps,
differing from the fentiments advanced by fome,
may, neverthelefs, tend to improve the elucidation of the contract between King and people; at
the fame time the meafures adopted at the Revolution correfpond with the fubfequent poftulate of
our focial compact.

We have feen that the Norman fyftem for a
time annihilated the free principles of the Anglo-
Saxons,

Saxons, whofe inftitutions form the bafis of our Conftitution, and that the people, by a variable exertion of their free privileges, under the tyranny and ufurpations of fubfequent Monarchs, were progreffively recovering and improving the Conftitution. Infpired with the free fpirit of the Great Alfred, whofe noble foul breathed that immortal fentiment preferved in his will, " * That it was " juft the Englifh fhould for ever remain as " free as their own thoughts." The nation waded through a fea of blood to regain his principles, † which, prior to this memorable Æra, were completely reftored fince their total abolition at the Conqueft. This circumftance enables us to judge on what ground the Revolutionifts acted. They had recovered their Conftitution of a limited Monarchy, and all parties feemed unanimous in that opinion, which is the only one fuperior to the contract between a King and people, which is, *That the Conftitution is facred and inviolable.* I do affirm there cannot be a doctrine more inimical to the interefts of the people than to affert, that if the Chief Magiftrate violates the contract, and forfeits the Throne, the Conftitution is diffolved, confequently all its inftitutions annihilated, and laws repealed. The contract on the part of the King is to adminifter the Conftitution as he finds it. " ‡ He can neither make any alteration or

---

* Hume, vol. I. p. 96.
† Black. Comm. vol. IV. p. 439—Charles II. 1679.
‡ Fortefcue, c. IX.

K   " change

" change in the laws of the realm without confent
" of the fubject, nor burthen them with ftrange
" impofitions." And as the law gives the
King his prerogative, and gives jurifdiction to
the Houfe of Lords, and limits the jurifdiction
of the Houfe of Commons, thefe reftraints on
the exifting conftituent parts of Government,
muft originate from the nation, when it had
reference to its original capacity of delegating
power, by political liberty, the laft recurrence
to which was at the Reftoration; and the
nation in its original character was at the Revolution, and is at this day, and for ever, legally
authorized to reform fuch ferious abufes in the
conftituent parts of Government, as amount to a
fubverfion of thofe powers to which it had primi-
tively given diftinct privileges, feparate forms, yet
a joint body, and concentred power, to be exercifed only for the public fecurity, the common
good and private happinefs of the people.

The firft power in the State is Political Liberty,
unalienable, always exifting.

The fecond power, the Conftitution facred and
inviolable.

The third power, the Three Eftates, as one
united body, fubordinate and relative, fworn to
adminifter the Conftitution with juftice and truth;
and

and in the legal difcharge of their duty, thefe powers are abfolute, and without control.

But in order to prevent abufes of powers fo tranfcendent and abfolute, each power forms a mutual check on the other; and the only fecurity the people have againft the Conftitution's being invaded is by the Third Eftate, their reprefentatives; and that fo important a truft fhould not be violated, wholefome * laws have been provided, which declare what perfons fhall be denied this truft; and laws are alfo provided to fecure the freedom of election. The facts on the face of hiftory, fince the Revolution, prove thefe laws to be inadequate; and the experience of a century fhows, that a reform in the reprefentation is now abfolutely neceffary.

From the reign of Elizabeth down to the Revolution, the Parliaments in general had acted with fo much patriotifm, and fo conformable to conftitutional liberty, that the public mind never fuggefted the idea of a reform in the reprefentation; added to which, the violence of parties fince the Reftoration had run fo high, that the Revolutionifts were content to facrifice future profpects of advantage by temporizing; and upon confulting the popular fentiment, they found it neceffary to compromife, rather than openly avow

* Black. Comm vol. I. p. 162.

-K 2

either

either their wifhes or the apparent neceffity of ftipulating for more extenfive advantages in favour of
Democracy, the factious fpirit of which had before
overthrown the Conftitution.

The great object of public concern was to limit
and afcertain the juft prerogatives of the Crown,
and to continue the fucceffion in a collateral branch
of the fame family.   And further, what was deeply
impreffed on the heart of every true Englifhman
was to fecure the Proteftant religion. In the Prince
of Orange were found qualities eminently adapted
to the important occafion, and whofe principles
were perfectly congenial with the Revolutionifts,
confequently he became the object of univerfal ado-
ration. The legality of his acceffion was in ftrict
conformity to the true principles of the Conftitution; to elucidate which I fhall affume an hypothe-
fis, and apply the fact to the principle. Pre-fuppof-
ing therefore the Conftitution to have been recovered at the Reftoration, and prefuming the reprefentatives of the people, at the Revolution, to have
been independent and true to conftitutional principles, the Conftitution may be termed a machine,
compofed of a number of wheels, one within the
other. The outer one, compofed of the body of
people, may be called the Wheel of Liberty,
which in its evolution communicates its powers to
the various internal wheels, till it reaches the
centre, which may be termed the Executive, or
the

Crown, whofe powers confift of a perpetual fpring
of action and re-action; but by deriving its active
property from the outer Wheel of Liberty, it is
virtually fubordinate to that, as poffeffing the original principle of motion; by which circumftance
the centre, or Executive Wheel, can never depart
from its fixed laws of motion, without infringing
upon the original one of Liberty; and as the primeval active power is inherent in the latter, the
remedy is alfo as well as the fupply of every defect. Hence the death of a Monarch can never
deftroy the Executive Wheel without annihilating
the machine. The confequence follows, * the
King in his political capacity never dies; and on
a parity of reafoning, an unprecedented vacancy
or abdication of the Throne cannot annihilate the
machine: for the perpetuity of the Executive
Power keeps the component parts together, till
the defect is peaceably fupplied, even when there
are no precedents or written laws to guide the popular mind. It is of the higheft importance to
the internal peace of the State, to the harmony
and order of fociety, that the Conftitution fhould
be confidered, under all contingencies, facred and
inviolable.

A Conftitution thus pure in its principles, and
equal in its parts, contains a primary intereft,

* Black. Comm. vol. I. p. 249.

which

which every member proportionably fhares. And one common intereft pervading the whole community, the theory of Government is rendered fimple, and eafily underftood. But the practice will ever require wifdom, founded on integrity, in thofe who direct its motions, which is the moft irrefragable argument for frequent elections and frequent Parliaments.

To compare this theoretical diagram to the facts which occurred, we fhall find them accord.

James II. had abdicated the Throne, and by that abdication the Throne became vacant and forfeited. By what authority did the Convention affume a legiflative capacity to fupply that defect? By recurring, *ex neceffitate rei,* to political liberty, the original power in the State, which bears analogy to the diagram ftated, wherein I have endeavoured to make it appear, that the perpetuity of the Executive Power keeps the component parts together, by a neceffary relation the whole bears to form one fyftem.

The application therefore to the Prince of Orange, and the Convention which affembled in confequence, and the feveral laws eftablifhed, were ftrictly legal and conftitutional, as further appears by the following precedents. After the death of William Rufus, Henry I. by flattering promifes

promiſes made to the people, was, by a Convention, ſettled on the Throne, to the excluſion of
his elder brother, Robert; and the confirmation
of liberties paſſed by him under the Great Seal
was held as concluſive as any laws enacted by a
Monarch in direct deſcent. And in the ſubſequent reign, Stephen was ſettled on the Throne by
ſuch another Convention, to the excluſion of the
Empreſs Matilda. And at the death of Henry III.
Prince Edward being then abroad, the nation re-
curred to political liberty, and without ſummons,
the Prelates, Nobility, and Commonalty aſſembled, and ſettled the Government till the King returned, and their acts were held legal. And in
the 10th year of Richard II. the Parliament ſent
a ſolemn meſſage to the King, that by an ancient
ſtatute they had power to depoſe a King who would
not behave himſelf as he ought, and be ruled by
the laws of the realm. And the Parliament convened for the reſtoration of Charles II. aſſembled
without ſummons, or authority from the King,
yet the laws which were then enacted were afterwards confirmed; ſuch Convention having aſſembled according to political liberty, the firſt principle of the Conſtitution.

The ſucceſſion to the Crown is limited, and
incapacities are attached to the legal poſſeſſion
of it, which render the inheritance a matter
of right in the nation, and not a matter of

right

right in any Prince, unlefs he be free from the
incapacities created by the people, and eftablifhed
by law. If this be not admitted, * a Prince may
claim the Throne, poffeffed of all the incapacities
which would render the intervention of the people
neceffary, by Convention or Parliament, to exclude him, and elect another from the fame family, whereby we learn a diftinction between a
right of inheritance and a right of fucceffion; for
there can be no right of inheritance in defiance to
the will of the law ; and † a Prince claiming the
Crown, by being next heir to his father, or other
relative, muft fubfcribe to the will of the law,
which alone can give him a clear right of fucceffion to the Throne.

The law is the expreffion of the general will,
emanating from the common agreement of fociety, fubduing the paffions by enforcing reafon,
and protecting the rights of men by difpenfing
juftice. Obedience to the law is the folemn pact
of the community ; and the fubfcription to its will
by a Prince, forms the compact between King and
people ; and fo long as his prefent Moft Excellent
Majefty, and his illuftrious iffue, maintain this
union, this facred palladium, free and inviolate,

* See the Refolutions of the Commons, 1681, to exclude
James Duke of York.
 † Black. Comm. Vol. I. p. 195.

they

they have an indifputable and unequivocal claim, and an eftablifhed right to the allegiance and fub-je6tion of the people of England at this day, their heirs and pofterity, for ever.

A further remark I fhall make, which will il-luftrate in an eminent manner the ftability of the Conftitution, which is, that the indivifibi-lity of the Crown, and the perpetuity of the Executive Power, preferve the component parts of the Conftitution in all unprecedented ca-fualties. If this theorem be not admitted, the Convention affembled on the abdication of James, affuming a legiflative capacity, and exercifing powers as independent of the people as they ac-tually poffefs when elected in a regular Parlia-mentary manner, might have conftituted them-felves an Ariftocracy, formed an Oligarchy, or eftablifhed a Republic; and having in pay the army and navy, and in poffeffion of the Treafury and Public Offices, the refiftance of a people inti-midated by Popery, and depreffed by the recent civil wars, might have been checked effectually; and a tyranny fubftituted on Proteftant faith might have reconciled fects, and fyftemized flavery.

But the ftability of the Crown, which is the fu-perftructure of the Conftitution, by that neceffary relation it bears to the foundation, which is the law, preferved the fyftem entire, that the breath

of

of Anarchy, or the voice of Rebellion, could not
reach it without annihilating the Conftitution.
The indivifibility of the Crown, and the perpetuity of the Executive Power, therefore naturally
dictated to the Public mind the fupply of the defect, without any innovation on the Conftitution,
or difturbing the harmony of the fyftem. For the
intereft which every man poffeffes in the community, is the beft fecurity for the prefervation of
this model of Government; for every individual,
by its abolition, would be deprived of whatever
right he may poffefs under the common law, whatever privilege he may enjoy from an Act of Parliament, and whatever franchife he may be par-
taker of from a charter. Under thefe confidera-
tions, the Convention of Lords and Commons
for the common good, and by the confidence re-
pofed in them by the nation, made the ftatutes of
the land and the principles of the Conftitution the
rule of their conduct, equally binding themfelves
as the whole community, from which deductions it
is evident that the confidence of the people is the
bafis of a Convention or Parliament, and a free
and independent Parliament the bafis of freedom.

To conclude thefe remarks on political liberty,
let it be remembered, as it ftands upon record,
That the people owe every thing they deem excellent and ineftimable in their Conftitution to the
exercife of political liberty; not one law of
liberty

liberty in the whole code, from the Invafion down to the Revolution, proceeds from the voluntary effufion of a patriotic heart in the breaft of a Monarch. The pride of human nature induces them to look one way, fawning courtiers another; and it is feldom the people can catch a glance. And notwithftanding, by the Conftitution *, whatever is exceptionable in the conduct of public affairs, is not to be imputed to a King, nor is he anfwerable for it perfonally to his people; yet when a weak and bad man fucceeds to the Throne, he muft be confidered as a neceffary evil; but when a wife and good man afcends the Throne, his reign proves an age of triumph, of freedom, and happy Government. It is not in the power of a nation by election to choofe a fucceffion of wife and good men. In all elections it is in general found, that intereft fupplants merit. The order of Nature muft be reverfed to command virtue and wifdom in a fingle man, or body of men; and the chance of good men by hereditary defcent is equal to that of choice, and never attended with its evils, rivalfhip and anarchy.

To imagine that Government does not confift of the various affections of men, is miftaking the nature of it. In every age it has proved as verfatile as man, operating alternately by paffion, pro-

* Black. Comm. vol. I. p. 246,

fufion,

fufion, and economy; by fear, folly, and wifdom, arbitrary and free. Let the warmeft Republican lay his hand on his breaft, and diveft his heart of predatory views, and chufe what period of the feventeen hundred years of the English hiftory he would wifh to return to; and let the ftrongeft advocate for hereditary claims and hereditary rights diveft his heart of the thirft of power, traverfe the fame period, and fix the data for the perfection of the Conftitution: England was never more fplendid by opulence, or more inexhauftible in refources, than at the prefent day; and the Conftitution, for that very reafon, never more liable to be perverted. But to the glory of Britain, the chief excellence of her conftitution confifts in being open to improvement. It is a folid machine whofe greateft beauty is to court furvey; it folicits inveftigation; political liberty gave it fpirit and motion; and that fame native power can ever maintain that which it founded.

SECTION

SECTION VII.

The Rights of Englishmen ; or, The British Constitution.

TO avoid a labyrinth of discussion, by adducing codes of law, and citing a multitude of authors, I shall sum up these sacred Palladiums under a few heads.

THE ABSOLUTE GENERAL RIGHT OF ENGLISHMEN.

POLITICAL LIBERTY.

Which is the supreme power of the people, or the right of convening at all times to maintain and preserve the Constitution and Laws, which guaranty their absolute personal rights.

THE ABSOLUTE PERSONAL RIGHTS OF ENGLISHMEN.

1st. The right of personal security, or the legal uninterrupted enjoyment of life, limbs, body, health, and reputation.

2d. The

2d. The perſonal liberty of individuals, which conſiſts in the power of loco-motion, of changing ſituation, or moving to whatſoever place a perſon's inclination may direct, without impriſonment or reſtraint, unleſs by due courſe of law; as by Magna Charta " no freeman ſhall be taken or impriſoned " but by the lawful judgment of his equals or the " law of the land."

3d. The abſolute right of property, which con-ſiſts in the free uſe, enjoyment, and diſpoſal of all his acquiſitions, without any control or dimi-nution ſave only by the law of the land, which was alſo confirmed by Magna Charta, which de-clares, " That no freeman ſhall be diſſeized or " diveſted of his freehold, or of his liberties, or " free cuſtoms, but by the judgment of his peers " or by the laws of the land." And by various ſubſequent ſtatutes, the property of the ſubject was moſt firmly ſecured. The obtaining theſe ſta-tutes was a legal conqueſt over Norman deſpo-tiſm. Theſe acts declare *, That no ſubject of " England ſhall be conſtrained to pay aids or " taxes even for the defence of the realm, or the " ſupport of Government, but ſuch as are im-" poſed by *his own conſent, or that of his Repreſen-* " *tatives in Parliament.*"

* Blackſtone, vol. I. p. 140.

THE

THE PECULIAR INHERITANCES OF ENGLISHMEN;

OR,

BRITISH CIVIL LIBERTIES.

1ſt. The three eſtates, King, Lords, and Commons, each poſſeſſing diſtinct privileges, and each eſtate ſubordinate to the law, which guaranties the common intereſt of the community.

" * The executive power of the laws being
" lodged in a ſingle perſon, they have all the ad-
" vantages of ſtrength and diſpatch that are to be
" found in the moſt abſolute Monarchy; and as
" the Legiſlature of the kingdom is entruſted to
" three diſtinct powers, entirely independent of
" each other; firſt, the King; ſecondly, the
" Lords Spiritual and Temporal, which is an
" ariſtocratical aſſembly of perſons ſelected for
" their piety, their birth, their wiſdom, their va-
" lour, or their property; and thirdly, the Houſe
" of Commons, *freely choſen by the people from among*
" *themſelves,* which makes it a kind of Demo-
" cracy, as this aggregate body, actuated by dif-
" ferent ſprings, and attentive to different inte-
" reſts, compoſes the Britiſh Parliament, and has
" the ſupreme diſpoſal of every thing; there can

---

* Blackſtone, vol. I. p. 50.

" no

" no inconvenience be attempted by either of the
" three branches, but will be withstood by one
" of the other two, each branch being armed
" with a negative power sufficient to repel any
" innovation which it shall think inexpedient or
" dangerous."

2d. Freedom of Mind on Religion. Every individual may worship God as the pure sincerity of his heart dictates, without any civil or religious restraint whatever.

3d. The civil courts of justice, wherein, agreeable to the language of Magna Charta, Justice shall not be bought or sold, but right be done to every individual without distinction.

4th. Freedom of Election, and a New Representation every Three Years. N. B. The Septennial Act and the partial representation of boroughs, are violent usurpations on political liberty, and must be reformed.

5th. The Liberty of the Press.

6th. Trial by a Jury of Twelve Men, who are to give a general verdict on the matter of law as well as of fact.

7th. The Habeas Corpus Act.

These

These invaluable privileges were created or confirmed by independent patriotic Conventions, and
can never be surrendered or lost but by corrupt
Parliaments. From the wisdom of seventeen hundred years has resulted these several sacred institutions, which being founded on true equity, reason and the laws of God, comprise and form those
certain fixed principles of Government, by which
a community may attain the certain enjoyment of
liberty, order, and prosperity; and no delegated
power, even the nation itself, cannot abrogate
them without committing a criminal act, by which
true equity and reason would be sacrificed, and
the laws of God be violated; for every nation in
the world, in the full and free possession of these
several institutions, must enjoy the highest possible
degree of human liberty. It is these which com-
pose the Englishman's freehold, of which the
King and Peers are the trustees, and the Commons
are tenants at will; to admit they have the power
to alienate or waste is no defeasance of the nation's
right of inheritance; the mind of man is above
the reach of law; and it does not follow that
power cannot be abused. We may as well affirm, that men having the plain precepts of
Scripture to refer to, shall invariably act virtu-
ously; but practice will constantly be at variance
with theory, as the profession of morality in the
gross by any power is dashed with the leven of
knavery.

L   The

The unremitting duty of Englishmen is there-fore to be vigilant, and with a patriotic eye watch every motion of Government.. If these sacred in-stitutions should be attempted to be perverted, a faithful spirited remonstrance should be laid before the Legislature. If they should be actually vio-lated, and this remonstrance disregarded, the people must have resort to political liberty.

The mutability and fallibility of man render, by a natural consequence, all human actions imperfect, whether in an individual person or body corporate, from which we may infer, that though it be possible the principles of a Constitution may be perfect, the administration of them may not. The Three Estates, the civil courts, and the various institu-tions, form a Constitution, which, figuratively speaking, may be termed an adamantine edifice, which through ages will continue the same, but in every age it will be inhabited by men various in disposition and ability, and versatile by the fa-shion of the times; yet every succeeding age will be at no loss to find the great outlines, the pillars and bulwarks of the mansion. And if a preceding age has ventured on useless or pernicious altera-tions, a succeeding age has a complete and full power to restore it to its primitive state. The abuse in the national representation comes under this de-scription; but as virtue and vice seem to keep an equal pace, and wisdom is partial in her favours, we we cannot reckon on a greater harveft of integrity or abilities than what a former age has enjoyed; and we may truly repeat, it is poffible a Conftitution may be perfect, though the adminiftration of it be not; confequently the Government, which is the operative power of the Conftitution, will ever be fhort of perfection, unlefs an adminiftration fhall fortunately be fo formed, that every member of it fhall have united in his perfon both integrity and wifdom. But it is the common misfortune of Adminiftrations to confift of men who poffefs wifdom, but are deficient in patriotic integrity. Hence a Conftitution founded on political liberty, often difcovers in its operative powers the principles of an arbitrary Government. The public mind cannot be too fully impreffed with this truth, which teaches men the extreme danger of imbibing from florid harangues on the perfection of the Conftitution a paffive moderation, and a total inattention to the motions of Government. Thank God, a majority of the nation is not in this dream, fatal would it otherwife be; for the time would arrive when the people would awaken fettered with the chains of arbitrary power. Difinterefted men, whofe principles are proof againft the immoderate thirft of place and power, whofe integrity regulates their ambition, will ever look with a jealous eye to the motions of Government; impreffed with the native principle of political liberty, they will ever conduct themfelves in a cool

L 2   intrepid

intrepid manner; their exertions will ever be conftitutional, and carry a weight and importance
very different from the fpurious abortive fpirit of
faction, which, from the nature of its predatory
principles, the energy of the Executive Power of
the Conftitution will ever fupprefs. But the true
fpirit of liberty will be heard; the people muft
renounce their birth-rights ere the Conftitution
can fuffer, or the laws be materially violated.

The Republicans who affirm that we have no
Conftitution, in order to accomplifh their predatory principles, may in this brief Section fee their
refutation. Thefe adventurers bear a malicious
envy to this ifland, which, from the eulogies beftowed on it by ancient and modern writers, we
find is reprefented as the " Granary of the Wef-
" tern World, the feat of Ceres; that its vallies
" are like Eden; its hills like Lebanon; its
" fprings as Pifgah, and its rivers like Jordan;
" that it is a paradife of pleafure, and the garden
" of God."

SECTION

SECTION VIII.

Remarks on the present State of the Elective Power of the People, and the Constitution of Parliament.

The distempers of monarchy were the great subjects of apprehension and redress in the last century; in this the distempers
of parliament.

BURKE.

IN an inquiry into the present state of the representation of the people, decency cannot be
sacrificed at the shrine of truth, if it shall appear
that the interests of a whole community have demanded a free discussion; and candour will admit
what impartiality naturally induces—a distinction
between the mode by which the popular representation is constituted, and the qualifications and
abilities of the present members.

When the love of pleasure and dissipation is dif-
fusing itself in an unprecedented manner through
all ranks of people, and the religion of the established church is too evidently losing its sanctity and
force on the minds of the great; men, whose passions are not seduced by a musical age, and whose
judgments are not biassed by the refinement of the
arts, will regard the rise and fall of nations; they

L 3 will

will find that luxury gratifies the paſſions at the expence of acknowledged principles; and knowing the mutability of the very beſt governments, with becoming zeal and reſolution, will exert their moſt ſpirited endeavours to ſecure the Freedom of Election and the Independence of Parliament, which are confeſſedly the bulwarks of their own. In fine, the people have been repeatedly told they have no other ſecurity for their freedom. It was a known apothegm of the great Lord Treaſury Burleigh, *That England could never be ruined but by a parliament. And when we are told by a great modern ſtateſman, "that the diſtempers of monarchy were "the great ſubjects of redreſs and apprehenſion in "the laſt century, but in this the diſtempers of "parliament;" is it not ſufficient to alarm every man? Is it not enough to rouſe the nation, to find theſe diſtempers ſtill ſuppurating. Without meaning to impute a ſhadow of apoſtacy to Mr. Burke, when he tells us, " † It has been the "misfortune and not the glory of this age that "every thing muſt be diſcuſſed," we are drawn into a painful confeſſion, that the Genius of Liberty has ſuffered an outrage, by one of her veteran advocates ſuffering his gilded day of honours to be eclipſed by the cloud of corruption, and leaving

---

* Blackſtone, vol. i. p. 161.—Sir Matthew Hale on Parliaments, p. 49.—Monteſquieu, Sp. L. 11—6.

† Reflections on the Revolution of France, p. 16.

the

the moft important fubject that ever impreffed on his heart, or agitated his mind, to a precarious dependance on chance, or the more doubtful fecurity of fecret and corrupt influence. In an exertion of his fuperior abilities, a reform in parliament is of all fubjects that alone which could add additional fplendour to his talents, honour, to his principles, or dignity to his name.

When we take a retrofpect of adminiftrations, to go no further back than the commencement of this reign, and reflect on the clamour and general difcontent excited by the fecret and corrupt influence of the *Butean* fyftem, during the adminiftration of a Grafton and a North. And when we now find an univerfal revival of this fpirit of difcontent, we muft be convinced ALL IS NOT WELL. And the reafon of every man muft direct him to the violation of the freedom of election as the true fource of grievance. The abufe of the reprefentation of the people has been and is the fole caufe of all public difcontents. And becaufe it has not yet been remedied, the adminiftrations of this reign have incurred the contempt of all wife men, the indignation of all honeft men, and the general execration of the great majority of people.

The art of governing a free people is the prefervation of that great chain in the order of fociety, which links, by mutual attraction and dependance,

the

the whole community. The balance of power and property, in the scale of equal justice and common right, is the great interested object of the people, and the business of government. The true balance of property is the necessary equilibrium in the Constitution, and the *status quo* of society: a brief investigation of this main spring in every free state, will enable us to decide more clearly the justice or injustice of our representation.

For the origin of property no certain æra can be fixed. The necessaries of life are the cultured or manufactured products of land. Various conjectures may be adduced to shew how and by what means particular men became possessed of landed property. Beyond a doubt, time out of mind and record, mankind have been divided into two sorts of inhabitants, the landholders and the labourers; and from the vicissitudes of human possessions, and the various fortunes of men, the labourers must necessarily form the multitude, and be dependant on the landholders, who are the few; and among these few there must exist relative connexions and dependancies, proportionate to their greater or less influence over the many. To balance these connexions and subordinations in a community, which are founded in nature, is the first operative principle of government. The balance of property has an intimate connexion with the local situation and nature of a country; it is not artificial,

cial, but natural; not fpeculative, but real. Hence
the Utopian hypothefifes of all levellers, from Pha-
leas of Chalcedon, from Sir Thomas More to Thomas Paine, being founded on the erroneous ground
of confidering the balance of property artificial; of
owing its exiftence to a legiflative power, and not
arifing from the conftituted order of nature, have
proved abortive. The balance of property having its foundation in nature, all fubordinations
among mankind have one mutual connexion,
and are linked together in one great chain. The
landholder cannot exift without the labourer,
no more than the poor without the rich. Every
man depends on his particular friends, connexions,
or his fervants, for every thing he may be faid to
enjoy. And this mutual dependance is a clear,
felf-evident proof that the Great Author of Nature
views mankind with an equal eye; by his immutable laws we owe our daily bread to each other.
And this actual ftate of mutual benefits fhould
ftrongly excite gratitude and fubmiffion from the
governed to the governors. And on the other
hand, it fhould be the daily ftudy of governors to
imitate the Great Author of Nature in his rich
benevolence, and in charity, promote and difpenfe
the bleffings of liberty, right, and juftice.

The conclufion from this reafoning fhews the
fcience of true government to confift in propor-
tioning all the parts of this great chain of connexions

nexions and fubordinations, that no one part fhould
fo interfere with another as to produce anarchy or
oppreffion. And from thefe remarks it follows, that
according to the mutual dependance and recipro-
city of action in the conftituent parts of our Conftitution, the Houfe of Commons, compofed of the
reprefentatives of the people, fhould be the reprefentatives of the labourers againft the landholders,
or in other words, the poor and the commercial
part againft the rich and powerful, to conftitute
the balance of property in the fcale of power.
Here the argument bottoms. This is the bafis on
which the Conftitution is erected. And this principle is general and univerfal in the ftate. And
every government operating on this firft and natural ground of thofe connexions and fubordinations, which form the great chain of fociety, is a
government of truth, of equal juftice, and of equal
right.

Upon this principle we fhall be able to examine
truly the different acts paffed at the Revolution,
and thofe enacted fince, for the freedom of election
and the conftitution of parliament. Of the ancient
manner of holding parliaments, we find it to be
the letter and fpirit of the Conftitution, that they
fhould be held once a year, or oftener if need were ;
which is the fame as they are held at this day. But
the great queftion for the prefent age to decide,
and which precedents of antiquity can have no
avail,

avail, is, whether a new Houfe of Commons fhall
be elected every year, every three years, or every
feven years? Or, whether, by the monopoly of
boroughs, members fhall continue to fit during
their lives.

In this review of the ftatutes we fhall firft notice
thofe relative to the freedom of election, in the order of fucceffion from the Revolution, and next,
thofe which relate to the duration of a Houfe of
Commons.

By the Bill of Rights, 1ft Will. and Mary, it is
declared in the 7th charge againft James II. that
he endeavoured the fubverfion of the Conftitution,
by violating the freedom of election. And it is
further recited, in vindicating and afferting their
ancient rights and liberties, that they do claim and
demand, and infift upon all and fingular the premifes as declared to be the undoubted right of the
people, the 8th of which was, that the election of
members of parliament OUGHT TO BE FREE.

This indefinite and equivocal claufe, *that elections
ought to be free*, argues either a compromife on the
part of the partial reprefentation of infignificant
boroughs, or an interefted regard to property. But
it is more rational to conclude the revolutionifts
had no other views than to eftablifh their religious
liberties on true proteftant principles, and to limit
the

the exceffive prerogatives of the crown; they never
entertained an idea of eftablifhing an equal and general reprefentation; and the Revolution in this refpect
was left as incomplete as thofe whofe heads ran high
with intemperate ambition could wifh. And this
want of forefight or neglect was no doubt occafioned by the terrors of anarchy. Their minds
were too much impreffed with the recent civil
wars, and the diforders of the Commonwealth, to
venture an extenfion of democratic power. They
were content * to keep meafures with prejudice,
which they deemed neceffary to the order and prefervation of their recovered Conftitution.

This conclufion the fubfequent ftatutes of 7th
and 8th Will. and Mary proves, which recites,
" That † whereas grievous complaints are made of
" violating the freedom of election, to the great
" fcandal of the kingdom, *difhonourable, and may
" be destructive* to the conftitution of parliament;"

* Mackintofh's Vindiciæ Gallicæ, p. 298.
† 1695, a fevere bill was brought in for voiding all elections
of parliament-men, where the elected had been at any expence
in meat, drink, or money, to procure votes. It was very ftrictly
penned; but time muft fhew whether any inventions can be
found out to avoid it; certainly, if it has the defired effect, it
would prove one of the beft laws that ever was made in England; for abufes in elections were grown to a moft intolerable
excefs, which threatened even the ruin of the nation.
Burnet's Hiftory of his own Time, vol. IV. p. 309.

for

for remedy whereof it enacts, that members, giving bribes of money or entertainments, shall be incapacitated to fit and serve in Parliament.

The positive tenor of this act fully proves the laws at that period; established for the freedom of election were not sufficiently coercive to preserve the balance of property neceffary to the free operation of the Conftitution. The weight of the aristocratic power over-balanced the democratic; and the reprefentatives of the people have fince acted as principals, fpurned the relation which they bore as agents or deputies from a ftate originally organized upon delegated power; and by various fubfequent meafures have difpofed of the elective rights of the people in fuch a manner, as even to have made their conftituents the inftruments of their proftituted authority; or, in the words of Mr. Burke, " * The notorious infidelity and ver-
" fatility of members of parliament in their opi-
" nion of men and things, by an indifcriminate
" fupport of all adminiftrations, have totally ba-
" nifhed all integrity and confidence out of pub-
" lic proceedings, have confounded the beft men
" with the worft, and weakened and diffolved, in-
" ftead of ftrengthening and compacting, the ge-
" neral order of government."

* Thoughts on the Caufe of the prefent Difcontents.

The

The heterogeneous idea of different interests in a community as a body, has introduced practices the most pernicious to the one common interest of the whole. This common interest is the foul and spirit of the Constitution, and which can only be rendered general and effective by the concurrence of all the constituent powers, in their several subordinations, to this principle. But when any one man or party, delegated with those powers, considers himself or themselves allied to the community by a separate interest, and the narrowness of their capacities, or the sordidness of their souls, influences them to a mercenary conduct of making their own fortunes, or, by patronage, those of their friends, the order of society is violated, and the great chain of common interest becomes daily weakened by the corrosions of secret corruptions and party interests. Hence have arisen the mischievous distinctions of a Court and a Country Party, of Whig and Tory, of Ministerialists and Antiministerialists; which are the consequences of private interests opposing the real common interest of the people, and have their only true foundation in the abuse of the balance of property in the House of Commons, through the monopoly of boroughs by the nobility and hereditary members of parliament. I trust I shall prove no argument under the face of heaven can support such an unwarrantable usurpation of political liberty, and gross abuse of the rights of the people.

The

The penalty of the laft recited act merely goes to difqualify the candidate fo offending; no punifhment or penalty being inflicted on the electors taking fuch bribes. The remedy intended by this ftatute was therefore to remind the candidate of his patriotifm and his honour. But honour, though a facred tie, and the law of kings, was found to wear away in the minds of fome members; for a majority were obliged to impofe another tie on their honour, with a penalty on their reputation and property, by 2 Geo. c. 24. which recites, that " Whereas it is found by experience that the laws " already in being, have not been fufficient to pre- " vent corrupt and illegal practices in the elec- " tion of members of parliament." For remedy therefore of *fo great an evil*, it enacts, that electors fhall, if demanded, take an oath that they have not been bribed : and it is further enacted, " That if " any elector fhall take money, &c. as a bribe, or " fhall agree or contract for any money, &c. to " give, or forbear to give, his vote; or if any per- " fon by himfelf, or any perfon employed by him, " doth, or fhall, by any gift or reward, or by any " promife, &c. corrupt or procure any perfon or " perfons to give his vote at any fuch election, " fhall for every offence forfeit 500l. to be reco- " vered as the law directs, with full cofts of fuit: " and any perfon offending in any of the cafes afore- " faid, after judgment obtained, fhall for ever be " difabled to hold, exercife or enjoy any office or

franchife

" franchife to which he and they then fhall, or at
" any time afterwards may be entituled, as a mem-
" ber of any city, borough-town corporate, or
" cinque port, as if fuch perfon was naturally
" *dead.*"

In this ftatute the electors are made equally
liable to penalties with the candidates, and the dif-
abilities feem effectual and conclufive. But fuch is
the mutability of human nature, and fuch the deficiency of human wifdom, that no ftatute can be
virtuoufly framed but vice will overleap. And this
laft recited act being the laft ftatute for preventing
this evil, moral obligations are hereby found to be
ineffectual in binding men in their public capacities, although they would blufh to be fo detected
in their private affairs.

Next we examine the ftatutes paffed at and fince
the Revolution, relative to the holding of parliaments; the firft of which is included in the Bill of
Rights, 1 Will. and Mary, c. 2. by which it is declared to be one of the rights of the people, that
there fhould be *frequent* parliaments.

This indefinite claufe *frequent* comports with the
claufe before ftated in the Bill of Rights, which
fays, " That the election of members of parliament
" *ought* to be free." And thefe are very evident
and conclufive circumftances to prove, *That the*
democratic

democratic weight neceſſary in the Three Eſtates was
left by the neceſſity of the times, at the Revolution,
unequal and deficient, and which paved the way for
all the abuſes and grievances which have ſince ariſen.

To controvert this affirmation, the ſubſequent
Act of the 6th William and Mary, c. 2. will be
oppoſed, which recites, That *frequent* and *new* Parliaments tend very much to the happy union and
good agreement of the King and people; it therefore enacts and declares, That Parliaments ſhall be
held once in three years at leaſt, and ſhall have no
longer continuance than three years at fartheſt.

But this Statute, however concluſive in itſelf,
was but a mere plaiſter covering a gangrene; for
the freedom of election was left open to every mal-
verſation of placemen and penſioners, and to the
corrupt bribes of the Ariſtocracy; and by the Septennial Act this gangrene turned to an actual mortification. The body was conſumed, and we have
now nothing remaining but the ſkeleton of political freedom. This Act of 1 Geo. I. c. 38. recites,
" That by an Act of 6th William and Mary, the
" continuance of Parliaments was limited to three
" years, and declares grievous heats, animoſities,
" and expences, had been incurred by that Act."

Theſe conſequences followed from the repreſentation being partial, unequal, and monopolized.

Had

Had an equal and general reprefentation been eftablifhed, wherein the lower orders made choice of Deputies, and thofe Deputies the immediate Reprefentatives, thefe maladies would have been eradicated, and the Crown equally fecured. Inftead of which the Parliament affumed a power which the Members, by virtue of their delegated capacity, could not affume, without handing down to pofterity this dangerous precedent, " *That a number of felf-interefted men, calling themfelves the reprefentatives of the people, and conftituting themfelves a Parliament, by being proprietors or patrons of boroughs, and by the fecret and corrupt influence of the Executive Power, and other daring violations of the freedom of Britain, may pafs an Act for their own legiflative exiftence for life, or for a century, and the Conftitution, by fuch fubverfive meafures, may degenerate into defpotifm by an Act of Parliament, and the People of England become flaves by Law.*

This Statute further enacts; " That the provi-
" fion in the former Act may probably at this
" juncture, when a RESTLESS and POPISH fac-
" tion are defigning and endeavouring to renew the
" rebellion within this kingdom, be deftructive to
" Government, Be it enacted therefore, That Par-
" liaments fhall have continuance for the fpace of
" feven years."

The neceffity for adopting fuch a meafure is not convincing and fatisfactory ; and though it may be
justified

juftified on the ground of having a prefumptive tendency of better fecuring the prefent glorious family
on the Throne, neverthelefs it proved an invafion
on the Conftitution, and promoted State jobbing,
which has fince arifen to an actual trade among the
higher ranks; and further, it has been the immediate caufe of moft of the public grievances and
inglorious wars which have occurred fince that period.   There cannot remain a doubt but Triennial
Parliaments would have equally fecured the Crown
and Conftitution.   But prerogative, corrupted by
Ariftocracy, ever vigilant, faw the opportunity to
grafp, and patriotifm, intimidated by a threatened
civil war, yielded a willing prey.

The fpeech of a patriotic worthy Member, in
oppofition to this bill, is deferving of notice.   He
obferved *, " That the right of electing reprefenta-
" tives in Parliament was infeparably inherent in
" the people of Great Britain, and could never be
" thought to be delegated to the reprefentatives,
" unlefs they made the elected the elector, and at
" the fame time fuppofed it the will of the people,
" that their reprefentatives fhould have it in their
" power to deftroy thofe who made them, when-
" ever a Miniftry fhould think it neceffary to
" fcreen themfelves from their juft refentment;
" that this would be to deftroy the force of all
" their freedom; for if they had a right to conti-

* See Debates in Parliament, 1715.

M 2

" nue,

" nue themselves one year, one month, or one day,
" beyond their triennial term, it will unavoidably
" follow, that they have it in their power to make
" themselves perpetual. He further observed, That
" to say the passing of this Bill was not to grasp
" to themselves the right of election, but only
" to enlarge the time of calling new Parliaments,
" was a manifest fallacy; for whenever the three
" years were expired, they could no longer be said
" to subsist by *the choice of the people*, but by their
" own appointment. For these reasons he thought
" the bill *an open violation* of the people's liberties;
" or, to speak most mildly of it, a breach of the
" members' trust in that part which would most
" sensibly affect them, and of that ill tendency in
" its consequences, that as nothing but the security
" of the Ministry could make it at that time need-
" ful, SO NOTHING BUT A STANDING FORCE
" COULD MAKE IT LASTING."

Thirty Peers entered their protests against this Bill, affirming that new Parliaments are required by the fundamental laws of the Constitution; and that the Bill, so far from preventing expences and corruptions, that it would rather tend to increase them, as the LONGER a Parliament is to last the more VALUABLE a station in it must become, and the greater will be the danger of corrupting its members; notwithstanding which the Bill passed, though in addition to the opposition it met in Parliament, petitions were presented to the House from different

different parts of the kingdom, wherein the people declare they looked upon it as an attempt to over-turn the Conftitution.

The family of the Pretender being now extinct, and the prefent illuftrious Houfe of Brunfwick reigning triumphant in the hearts and minds of the people, this Act fhould be repealed, as an in-tolerable grievance, from which arife the following queftions :—Has not the value of boroughs been fo much enhanced fince this Statute was paffed, as to render the monopoly of them a matter of infinite importance to families looking up to the Crown for promotion ? Have not the rights of election in confequence been transferred from the confti-tuents to the reprefentatives, who are nominated and returned in fome boroughs without making their appearance, and the inhabitants and electors are as ignorant of their perfons and qualifications as the people of New Holland ? Where then exifts the popular branch of the Legiflature ? If men can, independent of the fuffrages of the people, fecure to themfelves a feat in Parliament during their lives, what fecurity have the people for their liberties ? as by fuch an illegal meafure men have the power of eftablifhing laws, and impofing partial taxes, which may principally affect the people and not themfelves.

The inference from thefe queftions is this, that the prefent Conftitution of Parliament is tanta-

mount

mount to an hereditary Legiſlature, which is the greateſt of all poſſible evils. Is this a ſpeculative aſſertion, or is it a fact? What can ſo incontrovertibly eſtabliſh its being matter of fact as this queſtion? Are not boroughs as naturally bequeathed to the heir as the very eſtate itſelf, and deſcend from wiſe men to fools, and from ideots to knaves, who are all indiſcriminately entruſted with the freedom of Britain, the deareſt inheritance and birth-right of every Engliſhman?

Theſe are truths ſo well known, that to have reference to matter of proof would be to inſult the underſtanding of the meaneſt Commoner in England.

The firſt motion made to repeal the Septennial Act *, it is worthy of remark, was negatived by a majority in which were 113 placemen and other officers under the Crown. And every motion of repeal and reform ſince that period has been negatived by the ſame influence of the Crown. The country Gentlemen, the ſtanch friends of freedom, and the only ſupporters of conſtitutional liberty, were unanimous for its repeal. Part of the ſpeeches of two of whom I ſhall recite.

The firſt worthy Member remarked, "Bribery at "elections, whence did it ariſe? Not from country "Gentlemen, for they are ſure of being choſen with-

* See Debates in Parliament, 1734.

" out it. It was, Sir, the invention of wicked and
" corrupt Minifters, who have from time to time
" led weak Princes into fuch deftructive meafures,
" that they did not dare to rely upon the reprefen-
" tation of the people. Long Parliaments, Sir,
" firft introduced bribery, becaufe they were worth
" purchafing at any rate. Country Gentlemen,
" who have only their private fortunes to rely on,
" and have no mercenary ends to ferve, are unable
" to oppofe, efpecially if at any time the public
" treafure fhall be unfaithfully fquandered away to
" corrupt their boroughs. Country Gentlemen,
" indeed, may make fome weak efforts; but
" as they generally prove unfuccefsful, and the
" time of a great ftruggle is at fo great a diftance,
" they at laft grow faint in the difpute, give up
" their country for loft, and retire in defpair. De-
" fpair naturally produces indolence, and that is the
" proper difpofition for flavery. Minifters of State
" underftand this very well, and are therefore un-
" willing to awake the nation out of its lethargy
" by frequent elections. They know that the fpi-
" rit of liberty, like every other virtue of the
" mind, is to be kept alive only by conftant ac-
" tion ; that it is impoffible to enflave this country
" while it is perpetually on its guard. Let coun-
" try Gentlemen then, by having frequent oppor-
" tunities of exerting themfelves, be kept active
" and warm in their contention for the public
" good. This will raife that zeal and indignation

" which

" which will at laſt get the better of thoſe undue
" influences by which the officers of the Crown,
" though unknown to the ſeveral boroughs, have
" been able to ſupplant country Gentlemen of great
" character and fortunes, who live in their neigh-
" bourhood. I do not ſay this upon idle ſpecula-
" tion only ; I live in a county * where it is too well
" known, and I will appeal to many Gentlemen
" in this Houſe, to more out of it, and who are
" ſo for this very reaſon, for the truth of my aſſer-
" tion. Sir, it is a ſore that has long been eating
" into the moſt vital part of our Conſtitution ; and
" I hope the time will come when you will probe
" it to the bottom ; for if a Miniſter ſhould gain
" a corrupt familiarity with our boroughs; if he
" ſhould keep a regiſter of this in his cloſet, and,
" by ſending down his Treaſury mandates, ſhould
" procure a ſpurious repreſentation of the people,
" the offspring of his corruption, who will be at
" all times ready to reconcile and juſtify the moſt
" contradictory meaſures of his adminiſtration,
" and even to vote every crude indigeſted dream
" of their Patron into a law ; if the maintenance of
" his power ſhould become the ſole object of his
" attention, and they ſhould be guilty of the moſt
" violent breach of Parliamentary truſt, by giving
" the King a diſcretionary liberty of taxing the
" people without limitation or control, the laſt fa-
" tal compliment they can pay to the Crown ; if
" this ſhould ever be the unhappy circumſtance of

* Cornwall.

" this nation, the people may indeed complain;
" but the door of that place where their complaints
" should be heard will for ever be shut against
" them."

The other country Gentleman, equally distinguished for his independence and patriotism, observed, " The learned Gentleman (the Attorney-
" General) has told us that our Constitution has
" been often varied, and that there was no time
" when it was such as we ought or would desire
" to return to. Sir, it is not to be doubted
" but our Constitution has often varied, and per-
" haps there is no time when it was without a
" fault; but I will affirm that there is no time
" in which we may not find some good things in
" our Constitution. There are now, there have
" been in every century, some good laws existing.
" Let us preserve those that are good; if any of
" them have been abolished, let them be restored;
" and if any of the laws now in being are found to
" be attended with inconveniencies, let them be
" repealed. This is what is now desired, this is
" what the people have reason to expect from Par-
" liament; there is nothing now desired but what
" the people have a right to, frequent new Par-
" liaments; and the right was established and con-
" firmed even by the claim of rights, notwith-
" standing what the learned Gentleman has said to
" the contrary."

And

And further he fubjoined—" Now, Sir, to
" return to the power of the Crown, which the
" learned Gentleman has told us was too much
" limited by the Triennial Law. I think I have
" made it plain that the juft power of the Crown
" cannot poffibly be limited by frequent elections,
" and confequently could not be too much limited
" by the Triennial Law; but by long Parliaments
" the Crown may be enabled to affume, and to
" make ufe of an unjuft power. By our Confti-
" tution the only legal method we have of vindi-
" cating our rights and privileges againft the en-
" croachments of ambitious Minifters is by Par-
" liament; the only way we have of rectifying a
" weak and wicked Adminiftration is by Parlia-
" ment; the only effectual way we have of bringing
" high and powerful criminals to condign punifh-
" ment is by Parliament. But if ever it fhould
" come to be in the power of the Adminiftration
" to have a majority of this Houfe depending
" upon the Crown, or to get a majority of fuch
" men returned as the reprefentatives of the people,
" the Parliament will then ftand as in no ftead, it
" can anfwer none of thefe great purpofes. The
" whole nation may be convinced of the weaknefs
" or wickednefs of thofe in the Adminiftration,
" and yet it may be out of the nation's power, in
" a legal way, to get the fools turned out or the
" knaves hanged."

It

It would be fuperfluous to adduce the arguments advanced on the minifterial fide of the queftion, as not one objection of weight was alleged, or one rational argument advanced, otherwife than the vague apprehenfion of Jacobitifm.

Thefe two fpeeches ferve to fhew the general fenfe entertained of this pernicious Septennial Act at the diftant period of near threefcore years, and whether the evils here deduced were or were not fully operating, is not a matter to engage our enquiry; fuffice for the prefent age to know that grievances had increafed, that corruption was increafing, and that the cup of evil has now overflowed and fpread over the land the *lava* of accumulated taxes. And when we confider how Paymafters, Commiffaries, Agents, and other fervants of the Crown, have been rewarded, we muft conclude they have rendered to Government an eternal obligation, and that thefe taxes are to fupport

" The debt immenfe of endlefs gratitude,
" So burthenfome, ftill paying, ftill to owe."

Among the many illicit practices attending the abufe in the reprefentation, there is one of a very fpecious complexion, as having a pretence to fupport a facred tie which every true Englifhman bears in his heart—*a friendfhip for his King.* Under the pretext of being the King's friends, Members received

ceived a douceur for the ufufruct of their voices, creating thereby a diftinction in the reprefentation of the people, and deftroying the confidential relation which ought to fubfift in its utmoft purity between the King and his faithful people; for a King to raife bulwarks, battlements, and caftles againft his people is a moft heterogeneous idea, and a miftaken policy in a free Government. A great and good King of a free people can have no enemies within his dominions but thofe of his own courtiers.

We owe this fecret and corrupt policy to the genius of Charles II. and it may fairly be faid to be practifing Machiavel's maxim in ambufh—*Divide et impera*—Divide the people and fubdue them. Intereft will attach a majority, who are taught by the influence of this maxim, that there is a tide continually flowing to Court, where thofe get fooneft there who fmoothly glide on the current of corruption. What fhark but will go with the ftream?

Further, the continuance of Parliaments for feven years rendered it an object of fome importance to the private intereft of a Member; for if his election coft him at moft 1500l. and he was receiving for the ufufruct of his voice the leaft proftituted fum, 500l. *per annum*, he would gain 2000l. at the expiration of the feven years he fat in Parliament,

Parliament, befides the privileges of being free
from arrefts and the benefit of franks ; and to obtain a qualification for this little *eftate and finecure*,
the following practice has been adopted by the
needy : to borrow deeds of noble Lords and Commoners ftrongly interefted in the different exifting
Adminiftrations, have them conveyed to themfelves on the fecurity of bonds, &c. then make
oath of having a *clear eftate*, to the amount of the
fpecific qualification ; and after taking their feat
re-convey the fame to their patrons, and then fide
on every queftion, and vote in every meafure with
the mercenary troop.   This circumftance, and the
monopoly of boroughs by noble Lords and Commoners, their contracts to return fuch Members
whofe principles they are certain of, their rejecting
others whofe integrity may be hoftile, their nomi-
nating and returning candidates independent of
their conftituents, are notorious facts, the moft
daring violations of the freedom of election, and
grofs contempts of the law, as well as inglorious
facrifices of Britifh liberty.

That thefe may not appear unqualified conclufions, I fhall produce the authority of a great and
wife man, not lefs diftinguifhed for his lucid and
folid reafoning, than that his deep refearches were
ever formed for the elucidation of truth. Mr.
Locke tells us on this fubject, " * If the Execu-

* On Gov. p. 2—222.

" tive

" tive Power employs the force, treafure, and of-
" fices of the Society to corrupt the reprefentatives,
" or openly pre-engages the electors, and pre-
" fcribes to their choice what manner of perfons
" fhall be chofen; thus to regulate candidates
" and electors, and new model the way of elec-
" tion, what is it but to cut up the Government
" by the roots, and poifon the very fountain of
" public fecurity? For the people having referved
" to themfelves the choice of their reprefentatives,
" as a fence of their properties, could do it for
" no other end but that they might always be
" freely chofen, and fo chofe, freely act and ad-
" vife."

Thefe baneful and ruinous practices were nur-
tured by the Septennial Act, and cherifhed by
that Prince of political corruption, Sir Robert
Walpole, under whofe tutelage they grew and
fpread, and during the American war had pervaded every fecretion of the State. Lord Chefterfield, in his character of Sir Robert, fays—" That
" he brought to perfection that fhameful method
" of governing by fecret and corrupt influence,
" which at this time both difhonours and difgraces
" this country, and which if not checked, and
" God knows how it can now be checked, muft
" ruin it."

SECT.

SECTION IX.

General Propositions for accomplishing an Equal Repre-sentation of the Commons of Great Britain in the High Court of Parliament.

IN laying down a constitutional rule of action to accomplish this grand essential point, I anticipate the favourable construction of every sincere impartial friend to the Constitution. But observation induces me to except against all its enemies, which are those who are for reforming every thing, and those who are inimical to every idea of reform, against every clergyman who cannot, with that worthy prelate the Bishop of Llandaff, lay his hand on his breast, and say with him, My religion and my politics reside in my heart; and also against the gentlemen of the law, and those under the influence of Government, who cannot join with the venerable Lord Camden in this rule of conduct, Let the letter of constitutional law prevail, and right be done, though pursuing the spirit of perversion be the road to favour and fortune.

Upon the subject of this Section, John Bull, who had paid me a polite attention since our last discourse, commenced the following dialogue.

John

John Bull. You have fully convinced me of a grand evil that is pervading the vitals of the Conftitution; but to remedy which, however defirous and ferioufly neceffary, is not be attempted but in a manner fuitable to the dignity of the firft kingdom in Europe, and in a way becoming a great and enlightened nation.

The Author. Impreffed with fuch noble fentiments, there can be little doubt but the nation could accomplifh this effential renovation of the Conftitution without difturbing the harmony of the fyftem, or encroaching upon the acknowledged prerogatives and privileges of either of the Three Eftates. The ftable fupport of the Crown and Parliament is the united interefts of the community; and the King's prerogative is beft maintained by the affections of his faithful people. There can be no hazard in his Majefty's trufting to the ftanch loyalty of his fubjects, by conftituting a free and equal reprefentation; and his Majefty would arife to the true fummit of glory, to that pinnacle of immortal honour, which no Monarch fince the great Alfred ever attained, if his Majefty, by virtue of his Royal prerogative, would diffolve the prefent Parliament, expreffing at the fame time his fenfe of their loyal attachment to his perfon and family, his affurance of their firm fupport of the conftitution and the univerfal opinion of their confpicuous talents

lents and fplendid abilities; but that in his wifdom he had thought proper to increafe the dignity
of his Crown, the glory of his reign, and the common intereft of the kingdom, by cementing on
a permanent bafis the facred relation which in
all purity and confidence fhould inviolably exift
between himfelf and his faithful people. To render efficient this happy compact, to conciliate *all
difaffection*, and to preferve the letter and fpirit of
the Conftitution by rooting out corruption, it was
his royal will and pleafure, and the anxious defire
of his faithful fubjects, that before he iffued writs
for a new Parliament, the Members of the late
Houfe of Commons, which now ftands diffolved,
fhould retire to their refpective counties, and he
would immediately, by virtue of his prerogative,
iffue mandates to the Sheriffs of the feveral counties, commanding the Mayor, Bailiffs, and Officers
of every city, town, and village in the kingdom,
to make returns of deputies from the inhabitants,
chofen in the proportion of one deputy to every
ten houfeholders paying fcot and lot. The deputies fo returned to the Sheriff fhould by him be
fummoned to the county town, and there elect ten
reprefentatives; and every county having in good
peace and order returned ten reprefentatives, the
reprefentatives of the nation fhould meet collectively in the Houfe of Commons, where, on taking
their feats, an oath fhould be adminiftered to every
individual, binding them to purfue only thofe ob-

N   jects

jects particularized in the oath, for which they were convened, which is for the sole and express purpose of organizing the elective power of the people, so that a free and independent reprefentation may be formed, agreeable to the texture and genius of our happy Conftitution, and that a Parliament might be conftituted, on the facred principles of liberty, virtue, and juftice; the laws of God, the rules of right conduct for man.

The national Convention thus legally convened, fhould be limited to fit no longer than forty days, which fhould be part of their oath; and having eftablifhed the reprefentation of the people on a univerfal, liberal, and equal mode, fhould fubmit the mode, and the future duration of a Parliament to the Houfe of Lords, which fhould be fummoned for the purpofe; and after their concurrence, it fhould receive his Majefty's royal fanction, and his Majefty fhould immediately, at the expiration of the forty days, which would diffolve the Convention, in the ufual way iffue his writs for electing Knights, Citizens, and Burgeffes; and the Parliament fo conftituted would to all intents and purpofes enjoy the fame privileges, and be fubject to all the ftatute laws relative to the fame, as if no fuch Convention had ever met, by which not an iota of the privileges of the Three Eftates of the Conftitution would be affected, but, on the contrary, its true fpirit be realized.

John

John Bull. The meafure which you have propofed meets my full approbation, but fuch a pro-
cedure would be unprecedented. Should not a reform originate with Parliament?

The Author. With regard to precedent, * it is a
maxim of our Conftitution, that the prerogative is
that law in cafe of the King which is law in no
cafe of the fubject. The King only, by the Conftitution, can convoke a Parliament or diffolve one.
If at the Revolution the King could, by virtue of
his prerogative, conftitute the Convention into a
Parliament, and that Convention affembled prima-
rily to preferve the Conftitution, on a parity of
reafoning, his Majefty can affemble a Convention
for the felf-fame purpofe; for his prerogative †
confifts in a difcretionary power of acting for the
public good, where the pofitive laws are filent.
What difinterefted man in the nation would oppofe
his Majefty in eftablifhing the freedom of election
on a permanent bafis? What man would deem the
exercife of the prerogative for the immediate benefit
of the people, ‡ for which it was created, a violation
of the regal power, or an infringement on the privileges of Parliament?

* Finch, l. 85.　　† Locke on Govern. p. 2—166.
‡ Plowden, p. 487.

John Bull. Permit me to remind you of some general maxims. Kings, it is said, are seldom inclined to compassionate their subjects, because they never intend to become men; and the nobility are apt to despise the lower class of people, because they never intend to become plebeians; and the rich are in general arrogant and self-interested; I am inclined therefore, from these reflections to despair of ever witnessing this salutary renovation of the Constitution originating from Court.

The Author. Indeed, John Bull, there is something profound in your remarks. Upon maturer thoughts, I am myself in doubt, when I consider the strong barrier of self-interest which surrounds the Court, and stands in the way between the Crown and reform.

John Bull. I confess I was surprised you should think that it would originate from any other quarter than Parliament, which is the door at which the people at all times should have access, to make their complaints known, and have their grievances redressed.

The Author. I presumed it was well known throughout the kingdom, that so far as respects the subject matter, the door you speak of was double barred and treble locked, and private interest kept the keys.

John

John Bull. It is unufual for me to relinquifh an eftablifhed opinion on flight grounds; you muft apply fufficient evidence to enforce conviction.

The Author. All borough proprietors, great law officers, and members looking up for preferment, befides placemen, penfioners, and moft of the officers of the army, will oppofe this reform for an equal reprefentation, which is the birth-right and inheritance of the people. Upon the queftion you would find Gentlemen of the above defcription maintain a great majority againft it.

John Bull. Such a phalanx of interefted troops oppofed to the rights of the nation, confounds legal propriety, and renders hope defperate, I am convinced; but you have left me no refort, which is a matter of much concern to my interefts.

The Author. That a general reform in Parliament will originate with the higher orders in the State, I have my doubts. I am afraid it is too palpable it never will; the *lex neceffitas* will therefore eventually devolve on the people, and their authority will be founded on that fundamental principle of Government, *Salus populi fuprema lex.* Of this firft principle Sir William Temple obferves in his Effays, " The fafety of Princes and States " lies in purfuing the true and common intereft of " the nation they govern, without efpoufing thofe

" of

" of any party or faction ; or if thefe are fo formed
" in a State, that they muft incline to one or
" other, then to chufe and favour that which is
" moft popular, or wherein the greateft or ftrongeft
" part of the people appear to be engaged. For as
" the end of Government feems to be *falus populi*,
" the fafety or welfare of the people, fo the ftrength
" of the Government is the confent of the people,
" which made that maxim of *Vox Populi vox Dei* ;
" that is, the Governors, who are few, will ever be
" forced to follow the ftrength of the governed,
" who are many."

John Bull. Extraordinary recurrences to firft principles by the people, however well grounded and
fubftantiated, as the origins of every free State, and
authorifed by the law of Nature, of Juftice, and of
Right, are not to be called forth but when prompt
neceffity excites to virtue, and the fword to oppofe
the rigid gripes of defpotic power.

The Author. In admitting thefe primary laws as
the inherent rights of a free nation, and the legal
exercife of fuch general power, much depends on
time and circumftances. The meafure of oppreffion, and the degree of violation which the Conftitution may have fuffered, are not to be concluded
on and taken as detailed, but muft be univerfally
felt; and the nation can never be juftified in re-
forting to fuch general principles of jurifprudence,

to

to fuch an exercife of tribunitial power, unlefs the affectionate appeals, the faithful remonftrances of a loyal people have been trampled on at the foot of the Throne; and the patience of freedom has grown grey in the weary folicitations to arbitrary arrogance. It is then when liberty affumes what reafon dictates, virtue fanctions, and juftice obtains; a wife and benevolent King will yield in the firft inftance, an adminiftration fpurning the narrow fyftem of felf-intereft, will coincide when Royalty is difpofed to actions of glory; and by enlightened meafures and patriotic acts appeafe the public mind, and enrich itfelf with popular applaufe.

John Bull. You have explained the dernier refort to my fatisfaction; and a queftion arifes in my mind, if the prefent Parliament was to organize and eftablifh the elective power of the nation, the next Parliament following their precedent of affumed power might repeal what the laft had done; and in like manner continued innovations might arife in every fubfequent Parliament.

The Author. There may be a doubt whether a Houfe of Commons is vefted with powers adequate to reform the reprefentation; but it is the greateft of all popular delufions to amufe the public mind with the continued feeble efforts for this grand effential renovation. A general, manly, and confe-

N 4   quential

quential mode of reform, fuitable to the dignity of the nation and the rights of the people, is againſt as innovation, is inveighed againſt as perilous, fraught with danger, too hazardous for trial. There are three claſſes of men ſupporting theſe deluſive ideas, theſe ignoble reflections on a great enlightened people; firſt, the ſelf-intereſted borough proprietors, placemen, and penſioners; ſecondly, thoſe who not comprehending the nature and active power of Government, and not regarding either its mutability or its motions, while their own affairs go on proſperouſly, ſupport every Adminiſtration, right or wrong. The third claſs are thoſe who well know the preſent repreſentation was formed by partial rights obtained from Norman deſpotiſm; theſe are the impartial and moderate men who are equally the friends of the Crown, as the Democratic part of the Conſtitution, but are infected with ſuch a political cowardice, that however ſenſible they may be of the neceſſity of a general and equal repreſentation, they are abſorbed by timidity, and rather than amputate the gangrened limb, they are for applying palliatives. Hence ariſe all the partial and illuſive modes of reform. And further, what has ever over-awed a Parliament, and induced an imbecile attack on this perverſion of the Conſtitution, was the importance of eſtabliſhing precedents ſo unlimited as an equal repreſentation demands; they feel an innate conviction,

tion, that * " it is not in Parliament *alone* that a
" remedy for Parliamentary diforders can be com-
" pleated ; hardly indeed can it begin there."

John Bull. I approve of Mr. Burke's idea; and
I am convinced, if the prefent Houfe of Commons effected a partial reform, it would be a precedent equally unconftitutional as the Septennial
Act. It is a fubject of fuch magnitude to pofterity, that a legal Convention for the exprefs purpofe is only conftitutionally competent.

The Author. It is no impeachment of the authority of the Houfe of Commons to doubt its com-
petency ; it is for the benefit of pofterity it fhould
be held fuch. The disfranchifing of charters, and
the organization of the elective power of the people,
are tantamount to the folemn and public confirmations of liberties, by the Charter of King John
and Henry III. the Reftoration and the Revolution, which were by national conventions, and
by which were conftituted the reprefentation ; and
it is a folecifm in political argument to maintain,
that redrefs of grievances can be effected by the
authors of thofe grievances, or that corruptions can
be purified by corruptors, or that reformation in
any State can proceed from a body of felf-interefted and ambitious men, who are the acknow-

* Mr. Burke's Thoughts on the Difcontents, p. 100.

ledged

ledged abettors and supporters of the very infractions and abuses intended to be reformed. There
is only one mode, in my humble opinion, by which
a reform can constitutionally originate and be sub-
stantiated, and two ways to accomplish that purpose; the one, voluntary; the other by remonstrance, loyal yet firm, as founded on constitutional
principles. The first of these I have before stated,
the legality of which cannot be doubted; it would
be an exertion of the prerogative, founded on those
sacred principles which the body of the people it is
held does possess as inherent rights. If therefore
the nation has the power to depart from the express institutions of regular Government, when
those institutions have been violated, in order to
maintain its constitutional freedom; can it be
said his Majesty has not the same power to effect
the same purposes? As the guardian of the Constitution, he has an unlimited power in securing
those liberties which the law creates; but the wisdom emanating from the same law has happily
created a limited barrier, which prevents the Crown
from counteracting the power with which it is in-
vested. And if his Majesty was determined, in his
gracious benevolence, to trust to the stanch loyalty
of his affectionate people, his faithful subjects, and
promote an equal representation of the Commons
of Great Britain, the present Parliament could not
with any colour of justice oppose such a popular
measure. With this first proposition I shall conclude,

clude, That whenever the Government is agreed
on the neceffity of a reform, it never can be conftitutionally effected but by a national convention,
affembled by the prerogative of his Majefty for
that exprefs purpofe—Reafon rules the wife, opinion the multitude. If the torrent of opinion is
running inimical to conftitutional liberty, it is the
duty of Government to check it. On the contrary,
vice verfa, to promote with all its energy that glorious end. The general opinion now dictates the
neceffity of a reform in the reprefentation; that
opinion is a permanent fecurity, that if the meafure be adopted, it will be effected with peace,
harmony, and order. If the prefent Houfe of
Commons were to difcover fo much patriotic virtue and felf-denial, as to effect this falutary meafure,
no exception would be taken, altho' the precedent
be repugnant to the true fpirit of the conftitution.

If this voluntary mode be not embraced, a certain portion of future evils, from which we cannot
fay we fhall be exempt, as the very firft expenfive
war will incur them, will occafion a reform in the
reprefentation to originate from the people.

John Bull. I fhould hope the profpect of peaceful tranquillity will induce my Sovereign to give
me fuch a pledge of his facred attachment to my
Conftitution, as to render fuch a recurrence to political liberty unneceffary. But upon a fubject of
fuch

such magnitude, it is adviseable to draw from every source which offers. I should therefore be glad to hear what you have further to propose for the attainment of this great object, particularly as on your first proposal, we rather feed our hopes at the expence of our understandings, when we reflect that the private virtues of a Sovereign as a man do not necessarily constitute him a Patriot King.

The Author. In whatever relates to the maintaining of your constitutional liberty, I most chearfully comply. The measures which I have to propose will be grounded on the warrantable presumption, that if the sense of the great majority of people can be constitutionally collected, and laid at the foot of the Throne, a reform would be accomplished. Before I propose this mode a few reflections present themselves. The most undoubted proof of a wise Government is the peace, order, and unanimity of the public mind. A division of sentiment, and a disjunction of the common interest, are subjects of much import in society; for it can never be the interest of the Crown or the people to try their strength. Prerogative by an over-extension may, by the very measures it takes, work its own abridgment; and the people by a mistaken notion of liberty may endeavour to remove obstacles more imaginary than in fact, and by an exertion of their latent powers destroy the bond of union in the component parts of the Constitution, which may

substitute

fubftitute anarchy for order, confound diftinctions by loofening the ties of fubordination; and in attempting to be more than free, finally become enflaved. It is therefore wife, it is juft, it is prudent to adopt fuch meafures, that the whole community may draw together as one political body. The mode which I fhould recommend goes no further than to a rule of conduct fanctioned by law, whereby the people may maintain their conftitutional liberty. Hence the bugbear innovation muft yield to the more calm dictates of national prudence. The nation, in purfuit of this lawful object will preferve a facred reverence for the conftituent parts of the Conftitution, which are inviolable, particularly when the interefts of the people are fo intimately connected with its feveral inftitutions, and above all thofe laws of freedom which are the folid bafis of the whole. But thefe excellent principles of Government are reduced to mere theories, if the nation's elective power be violated. And can any thing be more repugnant to freedom and to the fpirit of our Conftitution, than to affirm, that the Conftitution of Parliament is perverted, and that none but the violators are competent to reform the abufe. Surely it is a reproach of the higheft nature to the good fenfe of the age, an age which rivals ancient Rome in the fplendor of its arts and fciences; an age in which knowledge is diffeminated through all orders of the State, when fuperftition yields to gentle toleration,

We need produce.

toleration; when commerce has fupplanted military ferocity, and the minds of men become civilized. It is impoffible to indulge a thought fo inglorious, fo unworthy of thofe truly independent country Gentlemen who muft be the principals in reforming this abufe. Such Gentlemen, both in and out of the Houfe, whofe conftitutional integrity is proof, who have large interefts at ftake, and who have but one common intereft with the people, by this reform will find their way to Parliament without expence, and beyond a fhadow of doubt will be as anxious to ftrengthen the arm of Government in every meafure relative to the interefts and honour of the kingdom as the venal tribe; a mercenary, cringing, fawning few, who never ftand upright before a great man; but from a natural bias of the heart, and curve of the mind, facrifice the public intereft for their own profit; equally infincere in their attachments, they dupe their fuperiors, and exulting in their duplicity, afterwards defpife them for their credulity; and having created a divifion of intereft between the Crown and the people, have introduced a fyftem of plunder. Nothing can refift this fyftem, which commencing with a treacherous facrifice of the common intereft, muft finally end in either flavery or anarchy, but the firm union of the independent country gentlemen and citizens, to effect an equal reprefentation, and eftablifh the freedom of election on a permanent and general principle. The

spirit

fpirit for a reform by natural confequence muſt become general; the people will fee their intereſt in it; abuſes will ſtill increaſe, and then they will feel the neceſſity of ſtemming that torrent which for many years has been widely ſpreading through the ſtamina of the Conſtitution, and looſening thoſe ties which ſupport the noble edifice, and which an independent Parliament only can preſerve.

A reform will never be effected unleſs adopted by a cool wiſdom, a prompt judgment, and a capacious mind, operating on a ſober extenſive plan. Every true Engliſhman, impreſſed with the value of his free Conſtitution, will make order his guide, and the public welfare his purſuit; and as I ſhould hope there is not one ſingle pariſh in the kingdom but what has ſome friends to conſtitutional liberty, and there can be none of that deſcription but who are advocates for the independence of Parliament, I ſhould propoſe that, to collect the real unbiaſſed ſenſe of the nation on this meaſure, a few friends to the Conſtitution, independent gentlemen, and citizens in every pariſh of every city, town, borough corporate, and village in the kingdom, in each of their reſpective pariſhes, without calling a meeting of the inhabitants, which might create diſorder, ſhould nominate one from among themſelves, who ſhould the following day go from houſe to houſe within his pariſh, attended by not more than two gentlemen,

and

and prefent to every houfeholder paying fcot and
lot a ·propofition for obtaining their right of
equal reprefentation ; and every houfeholder approving the meafure and the delegate fhould fign
his name· A majority of houfeholders thus approving fhould be deemed conclufive for a parifh,
and every parifh of every city, town, borough corporate, and village, having in like peace and good
order been thus confulted, a majority of parifhes
thus approving fhould be deemed conclufive for a
county. The delegates of the parifhes thus deputed with the collective fenfe of a county, fhould
by agreement meet at an appointed place, and ballot for one among themfelves to conftitute a national Committee of reprefentation, a majority of
counties having in the fame orderly manner deputed their reprefentatives, the national Committee
of reprefentation fhould affemble at an appointed
place, and felect from among themfelves ten perfons, according to the Conftitution, who fhould
lay at the foot of the Throne the collected fenfe of
the nation ; and his Majefty might be addreffed in
a conftitutional manner fomething to the following
purport :

After expreffing in the fincereft and warmeft
manner their duty and allegiance to his Majefty,
and their loyal attachment to his illuftrious family,
they fhould make known to his Majefty, that they
are

are a Committee deputed with the collective fenfe of his Majefty's faithful and loving fubjects.

To exprefs their deep concern in finding that all the ftatutes made to preferve the freedom of election, and the independence of Parliament, are rendered null and void by thofe circumftances, which in the natural courfe of things might have been expected from the partial eftablifhment of the elective power of the people, and the opening left for the fpeculation of private intereft.

To reprefent to his Majefty that the profperity of his Majefty's dominions wholly depends, under Divine Providence on a harmony between the Popular, Legiflative, and Executive branches of their excellent Conftitution; and they are convinced that nothing can preferve that profperity and uninterrupted harmony from the attacks of difaffection, or the underminings of vicious ambition, but an equal and free reprefentation, and fhortening the continuance of Parliaments.

To recall to his Majefty's mind the general fenfe of his faithful people on this fubject during the former part of his reign; that the obftacles oppofed to fuch an enlightened, neceffary, and beneficial a meafure were remote from his Majefty's gracious benevolence. The oppofition arofe from a number of felf-interefted individuals, whofe influence in the

O

Legiflature

Legiſlature can promote an armament to obtain preferment, or prolong a war to make their fortunes;
and theſe meaſures have been ſo adopted at the expence of millions of money, and to the loſs of
the lives of thouſands of their fellow countrymen,
to the high offence againſt the Divine laws and the
freedom of their happy Conſtitution, and which
have grievouſly oppreſſed his Majeſty's poor ſubjects, who are in conſequence labouring under the
weight of accumulated taxes, and the great advance
of the neceſſaries of life.

To humbly teſtify their affliction for theſe op-
preſſive evils, and to repreſent to his Majeſty, that
this alarming ariſtocratic power of the Commons is
the higheſt teſtimony that the Conſtitution of Parliament is violated by the defect in the repreſentation of the people.

To aſſure his Majeſty in the moſt unfeigned
terms their determination to ſupport his Majeſty
in his juſt prerogatives with their lives and fortunes; but that they are determined to reclaim their
conſtitutional rights of a free and equal repreſentation; that they will maintain inviolable the Conſtitution in all its branches pure and entire; and that
they will unanimouſly ſupport the dignity of his
Majeſty's Crown and the honour and intereſts of
the kingdom; and when the one ſhall be inſulted,
or the other be attacked, they will produce ſuch

liberal

liberal fupplies and extenfive refources, as fhall be unexampled in any former times for a defenfive war.

To reprefent to his Majefty's wifdom that the prefent fituation of Europe affures a tranquillity to his kingdom highly favourable to their demands, to the nation's immediate interefts, and to the glory of his Majefty's reign. They humbly therefore folicit his Majefty to exercife a prerogative fo wifely placed in his Royal hands, to diffolve the prefent reprefentation, and by virtue of the fame prerogative command a Convention fworn to the only exprefs purpofe of eftablifhing the freedom of election and the independence of Parliament on true conftitutional principles.

To affure his Majefty that they have maturely weighed every circumftance, have analyzed the effects, and anticipate the happy confequences; that they have taken in every point of view the interefts to be affected, the difadvantages it will be attended with, and the balance of power which will be attained; that in none of thofe circumftances do they perceive that his Majefty's juft prerogatives will be encroached on, or his dignity retrenched. On the contrary, the equilibrium neceffary for the free operation of Government will be conftitutionally poifed.

O 2 To

Finally, to reprefent to his Majefty, That in this their Conftitutional claim, they are prompted by that duty which every Briton owes to the maintaining of conftitutional liberty ; and in this their lawful demand, they difcharge that obligation which their anceftors entailed on them, which was, *To preferve the freedom of election, and maintain the independence of Parliament* ; and this they are bound to do for the immediate fecurity of their Conftitution, for the benefit of their children, and to tranfmit the liberties they received from their anceftors unimpaired to pofterity.

John Bull. The particular points of the addrefs are congenial to the fentiments of my heart ; my higheft wifhes centre in the great objects of a general and equal reprefentation, and the fhorter duration of Parliaments. It is impoffible his Majefty could oppofe a meafure required by the fundamental laws of the Conftitution, and fo neceffary for the fupport of its freedom ; that his Majefty could object to make his people happy and united, and by this meafure *conciliate all difaffection*, and render himfelf immortal honour, would be high treafon to fuppofe.

The Author. If the collective fenfe of the nation was in this manner delivered before the Throne, his Majefty and the Parliament would embrace the
dignified

dignified act, and in the plenitude of their wiſdom hand down to poſterity a Conſtitution, which
neither ambition could pervert, or injuſtice annihilate.

SECT.

SECTION X.

A Conſtitutional Mode of Reform.

The Author.

BEFORE we can enter on the particular mode of reforming the repreſentation, private intereſt, that powerful bulwark which ſuſtains the rotten boroughs, renders a few remarks neceſſary. A ſtrong objection may be taken to the *·mode of applying the public money to purchaſe theſe boroughs; for if they were disfranchiſed of their elective privileges, the proprietors might make them a better money property, by the increaſe of population and the revival of trade which would follow ; it being a notorious fact, that the decline of numerous boroughs is owing to the monopoly of noble Lords and hereditary Members, who poſſeſs every inch of land, to the excluſion of trade and manufactories; in conſequence, the ſurplus of population emigrates to villages, which multiply in every part of the kingdom, while the rotten boroughs are ſinking into contemptible ruin.   There are ſome exceptions, where a diviſion of intereſts exiſts in boroughs ; but in theſe the practice of

* Mr. Pitt's Propoſition, 1783.

building

building a number of fmall cottages, in order
to fecure the feat of a hereditary member, is
equally a grofs abufe of the Conftitution and a
reproach to the common fenfe of the people.
Such reprefentatives, in both inftances, confide
in the number of their houfes, and not in the
fair eftimation of the electors. Their tenants become their vaffals, and triumph over the independent few. Hence the men of real fubftance,
who are the fupport of the poor, and the trufty
friends of the State, have no influence in the motions of Government; and being juggled out of
their conftitutional rights, become the unanimous,
though filent abhorrers of that infamous fyftem of
corruption, which fubftitutes cunning and treachery for wifdom and integrity, which involves the
idea of a free Government with abfolute power,
and gives a flat refutation to the theory of the Conftitution.

John Bull. If proprietors of boroughs, by their
being disfranchifed, would be deprived of their annual rentals, in all fuch cafes, where private property yields to public benefit, an adequate confideration by the public fhould be given.

The Author. Moft affuredly. But it appears their
rentals would be benefitted by a reform; but I do
not attempt to affirm it would be equal to the dou-
ceurs from Miniftry; thefe are private confidera-

tions

tions and private interefts, which, by a perfonifi-
cation of the Conftitution, it may be faid to know
nothing of; it is totally ignorant of the poffibility
of fuch practices; it prefumes it was eftablifhed
for univerfal benefit, for one common intereft, and
not a partial monopoly. That every objection may
therefore be done away which is oppofed to the
disfranchifing of the elective power only of boroughs, let us for a moment confider the inroads of
time and fafhion. If the Conftitution was originally free, its vital principle muft have been a
fpirit of univerfal juftice, which no fubfequent innovation could derive the fanction of a precedent
from, if the ufage was inimical to that principle.
And at the prefent day, if true equity, reafon, and
general liberty, which the Conftitution is founded
on, renounces the ufage, that ufage is an ufurpation of the conftitutional rights of the people.

After the Norman invafion had defaced the
free Conftitution, eftablifhed by the Great Alfred, and annulled the * elective power of the
people,

---

* This privilege has been much contefted between monarchical and popular parties. But when we confider the difference
between military and commercial ages, and that the mode may
vary, but the principle be the fame, the difference becomes reconciled, particularly when we are undoubtedly informed the
Britons and Saxons were a free people, whofe Governments
were founded on the equitable principles of election; but on
this

people. The contefts for the Crown by the fucceffors of William the Conqueror, afforded the people
a partial refumption of their Saxon laws; and the
charters of various town tithings, or boroughs,
were renewed or granted to different Barons by the
different Monarchs, to fupport their refpective interefts, by which a partial acquifition of elective
privileges fpread through fome part of the kingdom, while other parts ftill remained deftitute, and
have continued fo down to this prefent day; and
we are ftill preferving the remembrance of Norman
defpotifm, by thus continuing the chartered elective rights of particular boroughs.

It would become a matter of enquiry, why the
now numerous and populous villages fhould have
formerly been exempt from a participation in the
motions of Government by delegation, when the

this fubject monarchical writers, as Dr. Stuart well obferves *,
" by founding the prerogative fo high, infer the abfurdeft con-
" fequences." Mr. Hume, who refts much on the authority of
Dr. Brady, an arbitrary writer, † doubts the Saxon Wittena
Gemote, or Parliament, to confift of any other order than the
Nobility. The *Principes, Satrapæ, Optimates, Magnates, Procures,*
which feem to fuppofe an Ariftocracy, and to exclude the Commons. In a few pages further he obferves, Security was provided by the Saxon laws to all Members of the Wittena
Gemote, both in going and returning, *except they were notorious
thieves and robbers,* which requires no comment.

* Stuart Antiquity Eng. Conft. p. 52.   † Hume, vol. I, 204 and 208.

inhabitants

inhabitants of thofe villages equally contribute to the public revenue as boroughs. If we were not informed that the civil diffenfions and wars oc-fioned the * great mafs of people to refide within the protection of cities and boroughs, every one of which was furnifhed with caftles for that purpofe. But with the abolition of the feudal fyftem, internal peace promoted a general confidence, population increafed and fpread, villages were formed, and with the introduction of commerce new towns arofe on the ruins of the rotten boroughs, whofe privi-

* " We know from Bede," fays a candid and manly invefti-gator into the antiquities of our Government, " That there " were in England long before his time twenty-eight famous " cities, befides innumerable caftle and walled towns of note, " many of which, though now extremely decayed or quite " ruined, were then very confiderable ; the greateft and richeft " part of the nation living in thofe times, for the moft part, " in cities, or great towns, for their greater benefit or fecurity, " and the greater parts of the lands of England in the Saxon " times, and long after, lay uncultivated and over-run with " forefts and bogs ; fo that the inhabitants of thofe cities and " boroughs being then fo confiderable, for eftates in land as " well as other riches, could not be excluded from having " places both in the Britifh and Saxon Great Councils. What " man of fenfe can believe, that the ancient and potent cities of " London, York, Canterbury, Lincoln, &c. fhould ever be " excluded from having any hand in the great confultation " about giving money and making laws, and for the public de-" fence of the kingdom in the Saxon times, any more than they " are now."

Dr. Stuart's Antiquity of the Englifh Conftitution, p. 285. Bibliotheca Poetica, p. 270. See alfo p. 272.

leges

leges retaining a * Norman aspect, the people found
it to their interests to emigrate from them, which
occasioned their decay.

John Bull. It does not appear to me, that any
rational argument can be advanced, that the one
common interest of the whole community should,
however long the usage, be garbled, cut, and divided into partial lots. If these partial elective
privileges can be vindicated by virtue of the Constitution, and be defended and maintained by the
antiquity of the practice, at this day, it is in
vain to talk of one common interest; it is a compleat defeasance of common right.

The Author. Fortunately for Englishmen, the
Constitution acquires its data from the Great Alfred; and its principles are founded on one common right for one common interest. The Norman invasion proved a paralytic stroke on freedom, under which every nerve of liberty became
torpid. In every age since that period, various re-
storatives have been applied to recover it to its primitive tone; but still, as that revered patriot the
great Earl of Chatham said, " It wants a new por-
" tion of health to enable it to bear its infirmities."

---

* One check to industry in England was the erecting of
Corporations, an abuse which is not yet entirely corrected.
                                        Hume, vol. III. p. 404.

This

This expreſſive ſentence of the noble Earl's was an evident alluſion to the partial and abuſed repreſentation of the people. Of the corrupt repreſentation of boroughs, at another time, he obſerved, " This is what is called the rotten part " of the Conſtitution. It will not laſt the century. " If it do not drop off, it muſt be amputated." And I preſume, by a further enquiry of the inroads of time and faſhion, it will appear that the nation may with ſtrict legal propriety adopt an univerſal and equal organization of delegated power.

John Bull. It will afford me pleaſure to have the uſage impartially examined. Truth will diſſipate prejudice, though ſhe had the army of Xerxes againſt her.

The Author. It is the virtue of common intereſt to have truth for its baſis. Your rights cannot be maintained without her. Endeavouring to continue therefore under her auſpices, I find there are upwards of * ſixty boroughs that formerly ſent Members to Parliament, among which are Doncaſter, Whitby, Kingſton upon Thames, Kidderminſter, Newbury, Blandford, Chelmsford, Tunbridge, Bromſgrove, &c. &c. &c. If theſe populous boroughs were to reſume their claims of repreſentation, could the Crown legally and conſtitutionally refuſe them ? In the reign of James I. Ayleſbury

* Brown Willis's Notitia Parliamentaria.

and some other boroughs claimed their conftitutional privileges. The Crown refifted thefe claims on the ground of their having been fo long dormant, but the plea was over-ruled; and if the above dormant boroughs were to claim in like manner, the Crown could not refift with juftice; for beyond a doubt every man in the kingdom who contributes his quota to the fupport of Government, has an equal right to elect with his neighbour.

John Bull. If the meafures you have propofed for a reform fhould fail, every one of thefe dormant boroughs fhould immediately claim their abfolute right to reprefentation, and conteft the point with the Crown.

The Author. A very judicious idea, as the legality of it carries with it the advantage which Hamden enjoyed in the conteft with Charles I.—the conviction of the public mind in favour of common right and common juftice againft tyranny and ufurpation. Upon further enquiry we find there are alfo upwards of feventy boroughs, ftyled fuch on ancient record, but which never fent members to Parliament fince the Conqueft; although they enjoyed conftitutional privileges under the Saxons, as town tithings, among which are Leeds, Birmingham, Stratford on Avon, Walfall, Kendall, Burton upon Trent, Macclesfield, &c. And it is worthy of remark, that at this day one of thefe

towns,

towns, Birmingham for inſtance, contains near
80,000 inhabitants, when the number of electors
who ſend to Parliament three-fourths of its members amount to but 41,000. And the face of
things is ſo entirely changed in the courſe of time,
that every argument in reſpect to the preſent elective rights of partial boroughs muſt fall to the
ground.

From Edward I. to the reign of Edward VI.
all the boroughs in Lancaſhire were frequently
excuſed by the Sheriff from ſending Members to
Parliament on account of their *poverty*; whereas
that * county now ranks with the firſt in England
for opulence and trade.

The

---

* Mr. Chalmers obſerves, in his Eſtimate of the Comparative Strength of Great-Britain, " That it is not too much to ex-
" pect, that Lancaſhire alone, conſidering its numerous manu-
" factories and extenſive commerce, is now able to make
" a more ſteady exertion amidſt modern warfare than the
" whole kingdom in the time of Elizabeth. The traders of
" Liverpool alone fitted out at the commencement of the late
" war with France, between the 26th Auguſt, 1778, and the
" 17th April, 1779, 120 privateers, armed each with ten to
" thirty guns, but moſtly from fourteen to twenty. From an
" accurate liſt, containing the name and appointment of each,
" it appears that theſe privateers meaſured 30,787 tons, carry-
" ing 1986 guns and 8754 men. The fleet ſent againſt the
" Armada in 1588 meaſured 31,685 tons, and was navigated
" by 15,272 ſeamen. From the efforts of a ſingle town, we
" may infer that the private ſhips of war formed a greater force
" during

The Merchant Guilds, or Charters, were granted to boroughs for the exprefs purpofe of promoting commerce and protecting trade. Can it in any fhape anfwer thefe effential purpofes, when noble Lords and hereditary Members monopolize every acre of land, and every houfe in their boroughs, whofe trade is utterly deftroyed by the decreafe of population occafioned by this monopoly? Is it confiftent with juftice, is it agreeable to reafon, is it confonant to the texture and genius of a free State, founded on popular reprefentation, that fome boroughs, which contain not a fcore of inhabitants, fhould have influence in the motions of Government by their reprefentatives, and other boroughs, fuch as Manchefter and Birmingham, which contain 150,000 inhabitants, fhould have no voice in the Legiflature.

John Bull. But it is faid the inhabitants of Birmingham and Manchefter do not wifh to fend reprefentatives to Parliament; they defire not the trouble of election; the jarring of interefts and divifion of parties might affect their trade.

The Author. If that be true, it is a very ftrong evidence of the entire change of cuftoms with time,

" during the war with the Colonies, than the nation with all its
" unanimity and zeal was able to equip under the potent Go-
" vernment of Elizabeth."

as

as elective charters were originally, as I before observed, granted for the promotion of trade. But I believe what they fear is the corruption and confusion of an election; what they despise and dread is the general depraved state of the elective power of the people. Otherwise, if they possess not the ancient spirit of their free-born ancestors, if they have sunk into a lukewarm moderation, a contemptible indifference, they are worthy of slavery.

John Bull. They say that they are well content with county Members; they have a pledge in their independence paramount to their grievances.

The Author. In every free State, the secretions of commerce pervade the interests of the landholders, and the produce of land and the increase of trade have but one interest; all borough representation may therefore be done away, and a free Parliament be constituted by independent county Members. But in that case, every inhabitant paying scot and lot, whether residing in a village, town, or city, should have a voice; and that the members might not be put to any expence, the inhabitants of every parish should elect delegates, and those delegates elect the immediate representatives; the election of the last might be compleated in a few hours.

John

John Bull. But in the name of a freeholder there is something so venerable, that the prejudice naturally attached to long revered characters would not reconcile the abolition of their elective power.

The Author. Very juft; I shall therefore offer you a plan for a general reprefentation, in which that refpected body shall still retain its elective privileges. With the freeholders I would include the copyholders alfo, who should vote for delegates, and thofe delegates elect the Knights of the Shire, as I am fully perfuaded a fair and equal reprefentation of the Commons of England can never be obtained by permitting every order of the people to vote for immediate reprefentatives to Parliament. Further, it will have this defireable effect, there never can be any long contefted elections, and the private fortunes of Members will never be affected by their laudable fervices for the good of their country. The prefent expence to which a Member is put, is not only an infinite difgrace to the nation, but an act of the higheft injuftice to the individual; and as fuch, Government is bound by every tie of honour and juftice to yield to a reform.

The freeholders and copyholders in every hundred or divifion of a county, I should therefore propofe, shall elect delegates from among themfelves in the proportion of one delegate to every

P   five

five freeholders and copyholders. The delegates thus freely chofen in every hundred, &c. on the day of election fhould affemble at their refpective county towns, and there elect the Knights of the Shire, which might be done in a few hours in every county in the kingdom.

This mode of electing Knights of the Shire would certainly accord with the original inftitution, which limited the qualifications of electors to the poffeffion of freeholds of 40s. *per annum*, to which at this day, according to the decreafe of the denomination of money, 40*l.* *per annum* may be confidered as not more than equivalent. The delegates therefore which the fmall freeholders or copyholders fhould elect within their refpective hundreds, I fhould propofe to be men of not lefs than 40*l.* *per annum* freehold or copyhold property; and this plan of electing Knights of the Shire, I truft, is eligible and conftitutional.

John Bull. I would be candid in ftarting an objection if any thing weighty ftruck me, I approve therefore generally, and hope you will fuggeft one as unobjectionable on the commercial part.

The Author. Your approbation is my chief aim, but in this I cannot promife the fame facility; for the variety of interefts a general reform in the reprefentation has to encounter, as well as the diverfity of opinions,

nions, the rooted prejudices, and a moft prevailing difpofition to nurfe old cuftoms like declining age, even when evils are acknowledged to be attached to the one, and difeafe has rendered the hope of life defperate in the other. Even though Nature influences the prefervation of the aged, and reafon tells us the continuing prejudicial cuftoms is wrong, yet fuch is the force of habit, that we che-rifh both with fentiments fomewhat fimilar. We remember the aged with filial gratitude, and a long continued practice infinuates a regard for the other. But the abfolute neceffity of a general reform ren-ders the diffection of the victim effential to confti-tutional liberty. Yet where fhall we look for men to begin the amputation, where fhall we find men fo difpofed whofe fituations in life juftly entitle them to the operation. It is to be hoped the good fenfe of this enlightened age will induce thofe to ac-complifh it whofe due province it is to render to the freedom of Britain fo defireable a purpofe, I truft they will embrace this peaceful opportunity and efta-blifh on a pure foundation the pyramid of liberty, as delineated by the Conftitution, and not leave the iffue to ftern neceffity or popular tumult. From a variety of plans for a reform in the reprefenta-tion, fome truths may be gathered, and a perma-nanent fyftem be produced. In purfuit of your intereft, John Bull, I am encouraged to fubmit one with all its exceptions for your approbation.

John

John Bull. I never expect to see a perfect system of representation; that mode, which being founded on constitutional principles, will assure the free administration of the Constitution to the people, is all that is required.

The Author. Beyond a doubt, the nearer an organization of elective power approaches to constitutional principles, the more eligible it will be; I shall therefore rigidly adhere to those ancient divisions and districts, the parishes, hundreds, and counties, unto which elective privileges were constituted by the Great Alfred, for the subordinations of magistracy, from the Throne down to the decennary, or tithing, or parish, which was a corporation of ten householders, who elected one from among themselves to represent and be answerable for them in the superior courts; and this principle of election ascended to the Eolderman, who was the chief magistrate of the county, and from him to the Throne itself.

The people of England, exclusive of Wales, are now computed to be about eight millions, who are represented in Parliament by 489 representatives; Wales sends 24, and Scotland 45, which make together 558. Of this number 369 are returned by 41,000 electors, some of whom are of the very lowest orders of people, while there are
thousands

thoufands who contribute largely to the public revenue, and have great interefts at ftake, yet have
no manner of choice of reprefentatives.

John Bull. But it is faid, that although a man
be elected for a paltry borough, he is declared by
the Conftitution to be the reprefentative of the
community at large; though he be elected by the
poor of a borough, he is equally the reprefentative of the rich.

The Author. Affuredly fo, for this reafon, the
terms of the Conftitution fuppofe the Members
independent and honeft, and the equity of law
fuppofes its operation cannot deftroy its principle.
But as the contrary is too often the fact, where is
the man who cannot perceive the fallacy of our
borough reprefentation? What fecurity have the
people againft a Member who will barter for boroughs? Will any man be fo hardy as to affirm,
that his conftitutional integrity will not fuffer by
the infamous traffic; it is a public fale and profti-
tution of an Englifhman's facred rights; and a
man who commences borough-monger, violates
every principle of human dignity and public honour, and is unworthy the name of an Englifhman.

John Bull. I am really afhamed to have taken
up fo much of your time on a fubject, the very

mention

mention of which muſt convince every man of common-ſenſe in England of its being an unwarrantable abuſe of the rights of the people, and a dangerous innovation on the conſtitution.

The Author. An innovation on the Conſtitution this practice moſt aſſuredly is, in the moſt unequivocal ſenſe; and yet, ſtrange to tell, the reform of this abuſe is held out as innovation—Innovation is the word ſet up *in terrorem.*

John Bull. I am ſatisfied the word innovation is made the ſtalking horſe of corruption. I beg you will therefore proceed in laying down a conſtitutional and temperate mode of reform.

The Author. The plan which I ſhall offer you will be to elect a number of repreſentatives on the commercial intereſt, amounting to the ſame of which the preſent Parliament is conſtituted. But that every houſeholder paying ſcot and lot, whether reſiding in a city, town, or village, ſhall have his ſhare in the motions of Government, by virtue of his choice of delegates, who ſhall elect by ballot the immediate repreſentatives.

Before I proceed to the organization of the counties, it may be neceſſary to notice the repreſentation of the eight Cinque Ports, each of which ſend two Barons, or Members, to the Commons
Houſe

House of Parliament. These privileges were
granted to the Ports on account of fitting out
ships against the coast of France, which appears
at this day, when the course of time has so enlarged the views of the different nations, and aggrandized their mutual strength by such powerful
navies, wholly unnecessary and void. From these
Cinque Ports therefore may be taken their 16
Members, which may be transferred to the large
maritime counties in the following manner :

Yorkshire is divided into three divisions, or
Ridings, East, West, and North, and sends to
Parliament on the landed interest two Members ;
but each of the Ridings containing as many acres
of land as some of our largest counties. Two representatives on the landed interest may be assigned
to each Riding ; therefore

To Yorkshire may be added	4
Devonshire	1
Lincolnshire	1
Northumberland	1
Hampshire	1
Kent	1
Essex	1
Sussex	1
Norfolk	1
Suffolk	1
Lancashire	1
Dorsetshire	1
Cornwall	1
	16

Thefe additional Members to be elected in the fame manner as before ftated for Knights of the Shire,

By taking the grofs number of inhabitants each county at prefent contains, the number of reprefentatives to the number of inhabitants are extremely difproportionate in fome, particularly Cornwall, Wiltfhire, &c. And to adopt an equal and adequate reprefentation of the commercial intereft, each county ought to be reprefented according to the number of inhabitants which it contains; and to regulate this without any innovation on their prefent diftricts and divifions of hundreds and parifhes, may be the moft eligible, as being conftitutional. I fhall therefore ftrictly regard thofe ancient divifions, and render the cities, towns, and villages, in fome meafure fubfervient to them,

The number of delegates which in each parifh within a county, whether conftituting a city, town, or village, fhould be chofen, may be rated at the proportion of one delegate to every ten houfeholders paying fcot and lot, The number of taxed inhabitants within a parifh to be afcertained by the parifh books; and the number of reprefentatives on the commercial intereft which the delegates are to elect, may be calculated at a ratio of five to every 100,000 inhabitants within each

each county; from this ratio will arife a number, which may be termed a contingent furplus, occurring from the organization of the county of Middlefex, which I fhall fpeak of in the order it follows with the other counties. This furplus may be added to the cities and principal towns, which will then continue to return the fame number of reprefenta- tives as at prefent, and others more only elected on this general plan, which I am defirous to render an equal and conftitutional reprefentation.

Upon the above principles of delegation, I fhall organize each county, adding their prefent com- puted number of inhabitants, the number of repre- fentatives which are now fent to Parliament, and alfo the hundreds and number of parifhes by which each county is divided. A clofe regard to the mi- nutiæ of figures is neither material or requifite. If a conftitutional reform be carried into effect, a true cenfus of inhabitants no doubt will be af- certained by accurate returns, and the number of reprefentatives from each refpective county will be rendered more ftrictly proportionate than a ge- neral computation can poffibly regulate.

BEDFORDSHIRE.—Inhabitants, 69,000—M. P. 4. The county returns two of these representatives on the landed interest, and the town of Bedford only returns the remaining two on the commercial, which at the ratio proposed are deficient to the number of people by one representative. This county is divided into nine hundreds, containing 124 parishes, and may be subdivided into three districts in the following manner:

1st DISTRICT.

Representatives

The hundreds of Wylly, Stoden, and Redbornstoke.— Every householder of every parish within this district, paying scot and lot, to vote for the election of delegates within his parish. The number of delegates determinable by a decimation of one delegate from every ten qualified householders; and the delegates of each respective parish, thus freely chosen to elect by ballot — at } the county town, Bedford   *2

This mode of delegating the commercial interest to be general, and operate uniformly within every parish of every district within each county in the kingdom.

2d DISTRICT.

The hundreds of Manshead, Flitt, and Clifton, — at } the town of Dunstable   1

3d DISTRICT.

The hundreds of Biggleswade, Wixamtree, and Barford, at } the town of Biggleswade   1

* One is added to this number from the surplus arising from the organization of the county of Middlesex.

BERKSHIRE.—Inhabitants, 104,000.—M. P. 9. which give a furplus of two Members above the propofed ratio, allowing for two Knights of the Shire which the county returns on the landed intereft. It is divided into twenty hundreds, and may be fub-divided into the five following diftricts.

1ft DISTRICT.

Reprefentatives

The hundreds of Reading, Theal, Faircrofs, and Kentbury, — —— at } the county town, Reading *2

2d DISTRICT.

The hundreds of Ripples Moor, Bray, Bernerfh, and Cookham, —— at } the town of Windfor *2

3d DISTRICT.

The hundred of Hormer, Oke, Ganfield, Farringdon, and Shrievenham, —— at } the town of Abingdon 1

4th DISTRICT.

The hundreds of Sonninge, Wargrove, and Charlton, at } the town of Oakingham 1

5th DISTRICT.

The hundreds of Morton, Compton, Wanting, and Lambourn, — at } the town of Wallingford 1

* To each of thefe numbers one is added frcm the furplus.

BUCKING-

BUCKINGHAMSHIRE.—Inhabitants, 118,000.—M. P. 14, which give a furplus of 6 above the ratio. This county returns two reprefentatives on the landed intereft, and is divided into eight hundreds, containing 185 parifhes, and may be fubdivided into the five following diftricts.

Reprefentatives.

1ft DISTRICT.

The hundred of Buckingham, at } the county town, Buckingham *2

2d DISTRICT.

The hundred of Aylefbury and Afhenden, at } the town of Aylefbury *2

3d DISTRICT.

The hundred of Difborough, at } the town of High Wickham 1

4th DISTRICT.

The hundred of Newport and Cotflane, at } The town of Stony Stratford 1

5th DISTRICT.

The hundred of Burnham and Stoke, at } the town of Amerfham 1

* One is added to this number from the furplus.

CAMBRIDGESHIRE.—Inhabitants.—145,000.—
M. P. 6, which are deficient to the number of
people by 3. This county returns two reprefentatives on the landed intereft, and two reprefentatives are returned by the Univerfity of Cam-
bridge, which return may continue. It is divided
into 17 hundreds, containing 163 parifhes, and
may be fubdivided into the five following diftricts.

1ft DISTRICT.

Reprefentatives.

The hundreds of Flendifh, } The county town, Cam-
Chefterton, and Staine, at } bridge — —*2

2d DISTRICT.

The hundreds of Ely, North- } the city of Ely — 1
ftow, and Papworth, at }

3d DISTRICT.

The hundreds of Chevely, } the town of Newmarket 1
Stapleho, Radfield, and Chil- }
ford, — — at }

4th DISTRICT.

The hundreds of Armingford, } the town of Royfton — 1
Southftow, Wetherly, Trip- }
low, Wittlesford, — at }

5th DISTRICT.

The hundreds of Wifbich and } the town of Wifbich — 1
Wifhford, — at }

* One is added to this number from the furplus.

CHESHIRE.

CHESHIRE.—Inhabitants, 147,000.—M. P. 4,
which are deficient to the number of people by 5.
This county returns two reprefentatives on the
landed intereft, and is divided into feven hundreds,
containing 87 Parifhes, each of which may conftitute a diftrict.

1ft DISTRICT.

Reprefentatives.
The hundred of Wirehall, at the city of Chefter — *2

2d DISTRICT.

The hundred of Namptwich, at the town of Namptwich 1

3d DISTRICT.

The hundred of Macclesfield, at the town of Macclesfield — 1

4th DISTRICT.

The hundred of Northwich, at the town of Congleton — 1

5th DISTRICT.

The hundred of Broxton, at the town of Malpas — 1

6th DISTRICT.

The hundred of Bucklow, at the town of Knotsford — 1

7th DISTRICT.

The hundred of Edifbury, at the town of Frodfham — 1

* One is added to this number from the furplus.

CORNWALL.

CORNWALL.—Inhabitants, 154,000.—M. P. 44, which give a furplus of 35 above the ratio. This county returns two reprefentatives on the landed intereft, to which number, being a large maritime county, may be added another, taken from the Cinque Ports. It is divided into nine hundreds, containing 161 parifhes, and may be fubdivided into the feven following diftricts.

1ft DISTRICT.

Reprefentatives

The hundred of Eaf:, — at the county town, Launcefton *2

2d DISTRICT.

The hundred of Kerryer, · at the town of Falmouth — 1

3d DISTRICT.

The hundred of Powden, at the town of Truro —— 1

4th DISTRICT.

The hundreds of Trigg and Pider, —— at } the town of Bodmin — 1

5th DISTRICT.

The hundred of Weft, — at the town of Lefkard — 1

6th DISTRICT.

The hundred of Penwith, at the town of Penfance — 1

7th DISTRICT.

The hundreds of Lefnowith and Stratton, —— at } the town of Camelford — 1

＊ One is added to this number from the furplus.

CUMBERLAND.—Inhabitants, 82,200.—M.P.6, which are proportionate to the number of people. This county returns two reprefentatives on the landed intereft. It is divided into five wards, containing 58 parifhes, and may be fubdivided into the three following diftricts.

1ft DISTRICT.

Reprefentatives

The wards of Cumberland and Efkdale, ——— at } the city of Carlifle — 2

2d DISTRICT.

The ward of Southallerdale, at the town of Whitehaven 1

3d DISTRICT.

The wards of Leath and North, —— — — at } the town of Penrith — 1

DERBYSHIRE.

DERBYSHIRE.—Inhabitants, 131,000.—M. ... which are deficient to the number of people by 4. This county returns two reprefentatives on the landed intereft. It is divided into fix hundreds, containing 106 parifhes, and may be fubdivided into the four following diftricts.

1ft DISTRICT.

Reprefentatives

The hundreds of Morleftone, Appletree, and Reppington, at } the county town, Derby   3

2d DISTRICT.

The hundred of Scarfdale,   at the town of Chefterfield — 1

3d DISTRICT.

The hundred of Winkfworth,   at the town of Afhborn — 1

4th DISTRICT.

The hundred of High Peak,   at the town of Bakwell — 1

Q

DEVON.

DEVONSHIRE—Inhabitants, 304,000—M.P.26, which give a surplus of 9 above the ratio. This county returns two representatives on the landed interest; to which number, being a large maritime county, may be added another from the Cinque Ports. It is divided into 33 hundreds, containing 394 parishes, and may be subdivided into the eleven following districts.

1st District.

Representatives

The hundreds of Wonford, Clifton and Exminster, at } the city of Exeter — *4

2d District.

The hundreds of Roborough, Plympton, and Armington, —— at } the town of Plymouth — 3

3d District.

The hundreds of Branton, Show-ell, and South Moulton, at } the town of Barnstable — 2

4th District.

The hundreds of Tiverton, Hal-berton, Haurudge, and West Budley, —— at } the town of Tiverton — 1

5th District.

The hundreds of Tavistock and Lifton, —— — at } the town of Tavistock — 1

6th District.

The hundreds of Fremington, Black Torrington, and Taw-—— —— at } the town of Torrington — 1

7th District.

The hundreds of Colridge and Stanborough, —— at } the town of Dartmouth — 1

8th District.

The hundreds of Shebbear and Hartland, —— at } the town of Biddeford — 1

9th District.

The hundreds of Axminster, Culliton, Ottery, Budley, and Hemyoke, —— at } the town of Honiton — 1

10th District.

The hundreds of Tingbridge, part of Hawrudge and Heytor, —— at } the town of Ashburton — 1

11th District.

The hundreds of Crediton Witheridge, and Winkley — at } the town of Crediton — 1

* One is added to this number from the surplus.

DORSET-

DORSETSHIRE.——Inhabitants, 146,000.——◄
M. P. 20, which give a furplus of 11 above the
ratio. This county returns two reprefentatives on
the landed intereft; to which number, being a large
a maritime county, may be added another, taken
from the Cinque Ports. It is divided into 29
hundreds, containing 248 parifhes, and may be
fubdivided into the feven following diftricts.

1ft DISTRICT.

Reprefentatives.

The hundreds of George, Tot-
comb and Woodbury, Pud- } the county town, Dorchefter *2
dleton, and Bere, —— at

2d DISTRICT.

The hundreds of Culliton,
Winfrith, Rufhmore, Haf- } the town of Weymouth and
lar, Rowbarrow, and Ugf-   Melcomb Regis —— *2
comb, —— at

3d DISTRICT.

The hundreds of Church, Be- } the town of Lyme Regis —— 1
nunfter, and Redhove, at

4th DISTRICT.

The hundreds of Cogdean,
Badbury, Knowlton, and } the town of Pool —— 1
Pimperne, —— at

5th DISTRICT.

The hundreds of Goderthorn
and Bridport, Tollerford and } the town of Bridport —— 1
Eggarton, —— at

6th DISTRICT.

The hundreds of Upwimfborn,
Redlane, Newton, and Cran- } the town of Shaftefbury —— 1
born, —— at

7th DISTRICT.

The hundreds of Sherborn,
Buckland, Whiteway, Yet- } the town of Sherborn —— 1
minfter, and Brownfell, ——

** One to each of thefe numbers is added from the Surplus.

Dürham.—Inhabitants, 100,000.—M. P. 4,
which are deficient to the number of people by 3.
This county returns two reprefentatives on the
landed intereft. It is divided into four wards, containing 84 parifhes, each of which wards may conftitute a Diftrict.

1ft District.

		Reprefentatives
The ward of Chefter, — at the city of Durham	—	2

2d District.

The ward of Eafington, — at the town of Sunderland	—	5

3d District.

The ward of Darlington, — at the town of Darlington	—	1

4th District.

The ward of Stockton, — at the town of Stockton	—	1

Essex.

Essex.——Inhabitants, 214,000.—M. P. 8, which are deficient to the number of people by 5. This county returns two reprefentatives on the landed intereft, and being a large maritime county, another reprefentative, taken from the Cinque Ports, may be added to that number. It is divided into 19 hundreds, containing 415 parifhes, and may be fubdivided into the eight following diftricts.

1ft District.

Reprefentatives

The hundreds of Chelmsford, Witham, and Dunmow, at } the county town, Chelmsford 2

2d District.

The hundreds of Lexden and Hinckford, ——— at } the town of Colchefter — 2

3d District.

The hundreds of Tendring Winftree, and Thurftable, ——— ——— at } the town of Harwich —

4th District.

The hundreds of Dengy and Rochford, ——— at } the town of Malden — 1

5th District.

The hundreds of Becontree and Havering Liberty, —— at } the town of Rumford — 1

6th District.

The hundreds of Ongar, Waltham, and Harlow, — at } the town of Chipping Ongar 1

7th District.

The hundreds of Uuttlesford, Clavering, and Frefhwell, at } the town of Saffron Walden 1

8th District.

The hundreds of Chafford and Barnftable, ——— at } the town of Brentwood — 1

GLOUCESTERSHIRE.—Inhabitants, 164,000.—
M. P. 8, which are deficient to the number of
people by 2. This county returns two reprefentatives on the landed intereft. It is divided into 30
hundreds, containing 280 parifhes, and may be
fubdivided into the fix following diftricts.

1ft DISTRICT.

Reprefentatives

The hundreds of King's Bar-
ton and Dudfton, Weft Bur,
St. Briavel's, Brideflow, and } the city of Gloucefter — 2
Dutchy, —— at

2d DISTRICT.

The hundreds of Crawthorn
and Minety, Britwells Bar-
rows, Rapfgate, Bradley, and } the town of Cirencefter — 2
Slaughter, —— at

3d DISTRICT.

The hundreds of Tewkefbury,
Tibleston, Weftminfter, Bot- } the town of Tewkefbury *2
toe, Deerhurft, —— at

4th DISTRICT.

The hundreds of Cheltenham, } the town of Cheltenham 1
Cleeve, and Kiftfgate, at

5th DISTRICT.

The hundreds of Longtree,
Berkley, Whifton, Bifley, } the town of Tetbury — 1
and Thornbury, —— at

6th DISTRICT.

The hundreds of Grumbaldah,
Puclechurch, Langley Wines- } the town of Chipping Sedbury 1
head, and Henbury, — at

* One is added to this number from the furplus.

HAMPSHIRE.—Inhabitants, 170,000.—M.P.26, which give a furplus of 16 above the ratio. This county returns two reprefentatives on the landed intereft; to which number, being a large maritime county, may be added another, taken from the Cinque Ports. It is divided into 37 hundreds, containing 253 parifhes, and may be fubdivided into the eight following diftricts.

1ft DISTRICT.

Reprefentatives

The hundreds of Buddlefgate, King's Somborn, Fawley, Barton-Stacey, and Mainf-borough, ———— at } the city of Winchefter — *2

2d DISTRICT.

The hundreds of Pontfdown, Bofmere, Titchfield, Bifhops-Walthani, ———— at } the town of Portfmouth — *2

3d DISTRICT.

The hundreds of Redbridge, Manfbridge, and New Fo-reft, ———— at } the town of Southampton *2

4th DISTRICT.

The hundreds of Eaft Medham and Weft Medham, — at } Ifle of Wight, the town of Newport } *2

5th DISTRICT.

The hundreds of Ringwood, Fordingbridge, and Chrift-church, ———— at } the town of Ringwood — 1

6th DISTRICT.

The hundreds of Andover, Thorngate, Wherwell, Af-trow, Evingar, Kingfclear, and Overton, — at } the town of Andover — 1

7th DISTRICT.

The hundreds of Basingstoke,
Chutely, Holdshot, Odiham,
Crondal, Bermondspitt, and } the town of Basingstoke   1
Michael Dever, — at

8th DISTRICT.

The hundreds of Finchdean,
East Meon, Meonstoke, Al-
ton, Selborn, and Bishop's- } the town of Petersfield — *1
Sutton, ———— at

**** One is added to each of these numbers from the surplus.

HARTFORDSHIRE.——Inhabitants, 103,000.——
M. P. 6, which are deficient to the number of
people by 1. This county returns two representatives on the landed interest. It is divided into eight
hundreds, containing 121 parishes, and may be
subdivided into the five following districts.

1st DISTRICT.

Representatives

The hundreds of Hartford and }
Broadwater, —— at } the county town, Hartford *2

2d DISTRICT.

The hundreds of Brogin and }
Edwintree, —— at } the town of Ware —— 1

3d DISTRICT.

The hundred of Cashio, at the town of St. Alban's — 1

4th DISTRICT.

The hundreds of Hitchin and }
Odsey, —— at } the town of Hitchin —— 1

5th DISTRICT.

The hundreds of Ducorum, at the town of Tring —— 1

* One is added to this number from the surplus.

HEREFORDSHIRE.—Inhabitants, 98,000.——M. P. 8, which give a furplus of 1 above the ratio. This county returns two reprefentatives on the landed intereft. It is divided into 11 hundreds, containing 176 parifhes, and may be fubdivided into the five following diftricts.

1ft DISTRICT.

Reprefentatives.

The hundreds of Grimfworth, Webtree, and Ewayflacey, at } the city of Hereford — *2

2d DISTRICT.

The hundreds of Wolphy and Wigmore, at } the town of Leominfter — 2

3d DISTRICT.

The hundreds of Greytree and Wormlow, at } the town of Rofs — 1

4th DISTRICT.

The hundreds of Radlow and Broxafh at } the town of Ledbury — 1

5th DISTRICT.

The hundreds of Stretford and Huntington, at } the town of Weobly — 1

* One is added to this number from the furplus,

HUNTINGDONSHIRE.—Inhabitants, 57,000.— M. P. 4, which are deficient to the number of people by 1. This county returns two reprefentatives on the landed intereft. It is divided into four hundreds, containing 73 parifhes, and may be fubdivided into the two following diftriéts.

1ft DISTRICT.

Reprefentatives

The hundreds of Norman Crofs and Huntingftone, at } the county town, Huntingdon 2

2d DISTRICT.

The hundreds of Tofeland and Leightonftone, ———— at } the town of St. Neot's 1

KENT.

KENT.——Inhabitants, 257,000.—M. P. 26, which give a furplus of 11 above the ratio. This county returns two reprefentatives on the landed intereft; to which number, being a large maritime county, may be added another, taken from the Cinque Ports. It is divided into 62 hundreds, containing 408 parifhes, and may be fubdivided into the eleven following diftricts.

1ft DISTRICT.

Reprefentatives

The hundreds of Bridge and Petham, Weftgate, Down Chamford, Kinghamford, Stowting, Bircholtfranchife, ————— ————— at } the city of Canterbury — 3

2d DISTRICT.

The hundreds of Shamel, Hoo, Milton, Ifle of Shepey, and Toltingtrow, ——— at } the city of Rochefter — *2

3d DISTRICT.

The hundreds of Maidftone, Larkfield, Eyhorn, Twiford, Rotham, Marden, Cranbrook, Barkley, and Rolvenden, ——— at } the town of Maidftone — *2

4th DISTRICT.

The hundreds of Bewfburough, Folkeftone, Loningborough, Heane, and Streats, at } the town of Dover — *2

5th DISTRICT.

The hundreds of Eaftrey, Cornilo, Wingham, and Prefton, ——— at } the town of Sandwich — 1

6th District.

The hundreds of New Church, Langport, Allowſbridge, Ham, Worth, Oxney, Tenterden. and Blackborn, at } the town of New Romney   1

7th District.

The hundreds of Blengate, Iſle of Thanet, Ringſlow, and Whitſtable, ———— at } the town of Margate   — 1

8th District.

The hundreds of Feverſham, Boćton, Felborough, Chart and Longbridge, and Tenham, ———— at } the town of Feverſham — 1

9th District.

The hundreds of Dartford and Wilmington, Axſtane, Godſheath, Somerden, and Weſterham, at ———— at } the town of Dartford   — 1

10th District.

The hundreds of Blackheath, Bromley, Beckenham, Rookeſley, and Leſneſs ——— at } the town of Greenwich   1

11th District.

The hundreds of Tunbridge, Watlingſton, Brencley and Horſmunden, Weſt and Eaſt Barnfield and Selbrittenden, ——— ——— at } the town of Tunbridge — 1

⁎ One is added to each of theſe numbers from the ſurplus.

LANCASHIRE.

LANCASHIRE.——Inhabitants, 260,000.——
M. P. 14, which are deficient to the number of
people by 1. This county returns two reprefentatives on the landed interest; to which number,
being a large maritime county, may be added another, taken from the Cinque Ports. It is divided
into fix hundreds, containing 61 parifhes; each
of thefe hundreds may conftitute a diftrict.

1ft DISTRICT.

Reprefentatives

| The hundred of Fournefs or Loynfdale —— at } the county town, Lancafter | 2 |

2d DISTRICT.

The hundred of Weft Derby   at the town of Liverpool — 3

3d DISTRICT.

The hundred of Salford   —   at the town of Manchefter   3

4th DISTRICT.

The hundred of Moundernefs   at the town of Prefton —— 2

5th DISTRICT.

The hundred of Layland   —   at the town of Wigan   —   2

6th DISTRICT.

The hundred of Blackburn —   at the town of Blackburn   2

LEICESTERSHIRE.

LEICESTERSHIRE.———Inhabitants, 116,000.——
M. P. 4, which are deficient to the number of
people by 4. This county returns two reprefentatives on the landed intereft. It is divided into fix
hundreds, containing 192 parifhes; each of thefe
hundreds may conftitute a diftrict.

1ft DISTRICT.

Reprefentatives
The hundred of Eaft Gofcote, at the county town, Leicefter *2

2d DISTRICT.
The hundred of Weft Gofcote, at the town of Loughborough 1

3d DISTRICT.
The hundred of Gartrey —— at the town of Harborough 1

4th DISTRICT.
The hundred of Framland, —— at the town of MiltonMowbray 1

5th DISTRICT.
The hundred of Goodlaxton, at the town of Lutterworth 1

6th DISTRICT.
The hundred of Sparkingho, at the town of Hinckley —— 1

* One is added to this number from the furplus.

LINCOLNSHIRE.—Inhabitants, 252,000.——
M. P. 12, which are deficient to the number of
people by 3. This county returns two reprefentatives on the landed intereft; to which number,
being a large maritime county, may be added another, taken from the Cinque Ports. It is divided
into 30 hundreds, containing 630 parifhes, and
may be fubdivided into the fix following diftricts.

1ft DISTRICT.

Reprefentatives

The hundreds of Lawris, Lin-
coln Liberty, Wraggot, and } the city of Lincoln —— 3
Gartrey —— at

2d DISTRICT.

The hundreds of Neffe, Ellow
Kirton, Aveland, Beltiflow, } the town of Stamford ——1
and Afwardburn, —— at

3d DISTRICT.

The hundreds of Grantham,
Wiverbridge, Loveden, Flax- } the town of Grantham —— 2
well, Boothby, and Lango, at

4th DISTRICT.

The hundreds of Skirbeck,
Horncaftle, Bullingbrook, } the town of Bofton —— 2
Candlefhow, Hill, and Calce-
worth —— at

5th DISTRICT.

The hundreds of Bradley, Lud-
brough, Louthcafk, Walfh- } the town of Grimfby —— 2
croft, and Yarburough, at

6th DISTRICT.

The hundreds of Corringham,
Manlake, Aflacote, and Well, } the town of Grifborough — 2
—— —— at

MIDDLESEX.——Inhabitants, 1,350,000.——
M. P. 8. The fmallnefs of this county, and the
immenfe number of people it contains, would
feem to obviate this mode for an equal reprefentation, as there is a deficiency in the prefent return from this county of no lefs than 59 reprefentatives. The county returns two reprefentatives
on the landed intereft, and is divided into feven
hundreds, containing 200 parifhes, and may be
fub-divided into the eleven following diftricts.

ıſt DISTRICT.

Reprefentatives

The city of London, from the earlieft periods of hiftory, has been diftinguifhed by privileges peculiar to itfelf, and on the mode propofed muft ftand an exception to the propofed ratio; for agreeably to that it fhould return forty reprefentatives, which is a proportion, it will readily be allowed, as much too great as the prefent number are too few, when its population and high importance in the State are duly confidered. To reconcile this objection, eight reprefentatives may be affigned to the city of London, to be elected in the ufual manner as the livery are in general, a clafs removed from the lower orders of people. } the city of London — 8

2d DISTRICT.

Representatives

The parishes within the liberties of Westminster to elect
on the general mode pro-
posed, by delegates returned
from each parish, which will
have this good effect, there
never can be again *an age* of
electioneering, or *an eternal*
scrutiny, and the inhabitants
will always have it in their
power to elect independent
and able men. ——— at the city of Westminster —— 4

3d DISTRICT.

The Kensington division of the
hundred of Ossulston — at the town of Brentford — 2

4th DISTRICT.

The Holborn division of the
hundred of Ossulston — at the town of Hampstead — 2

5th DISTRICT.

The Finsbury division of the
hundred of Ossulston — at the town of Highgate — 2

6th DISTRICT.

The Tower division of the
hundred of Ossulston — at the town of Hackney — 2

7th DISTRICT.

The hundred of Edmonton, at the town of Enfield —— 2

8th DISTRICT.

The hundred of Istleworth, at the town of Hounslow — 2

9th DISTRICT.

The hundred of Spelthorne, at the town of Staines ——— 2

10th DISTRICT.

The hundred of Goare, at the town of Stanmore — 2

11th DISTRICT.

The hundred of Elthorne — at the town of Uxbridge — 2

MONMOUTHSHIRE.—Inhabitants, 42,000.—
M. P. 4, which are proportionate to the number of
people. This county returns two representatives
on the landed interest. It is divided into six hundreds, containing 127 Parishes, and may be subdivided into the two following districts.

1st DISTRICT.

Representatives

The hundred of Skinfrith,
Ragland, Trelech, and Calde-
cot, — at } the county town, Monmouth *2

2d DISTRICT.

The hundreds of Bergavenny,
Wenlooge, and Usk — at } the town of Abergavenny   1

* One is added to this number from the surplus.

NORFOLK.—Inhabitants, 285,000.—M. P. 12, which are deficient to the number of people by 4. This county returns two reprefentatives on the landed intereft; to which number, being a large maritime county, may be added another, taken from the Cinque Ports. It is divided into 31 hundreds, containing 660 parifhes, and may be fubdivided into the eleven following diftricts.

1ft DISTRICT.

Reprefentatives

The hundreds of Taverham, Blowfield, and Humbleyard, at } the city of Norwich — *4

2d DISTRICT.

The hundreds of Grimfhoe, Shropeham, and Gilecrofs, at } the town of Thetford — 2

3d DISTRICT.

The hundreds of Eaft Flegg, Weft Flegg, and Walfham, at } the town of Yarmouth — 2

4th DISTRICT.

The hundreds of Freebridge and Clackclofe — at } the town of Lynn Regis — 1

5th DISTRICT.

The hundreds of Greenhoe, Wayland, and Laundich, at } the town of Swaffham — 1

6th DISTRICT.

The hundreds of Foreho, Milford, and Eynsford — at } the town of Wymondham 1

7th DI-

7th DISTRICT.

Reprefentatives

The hundreds of North Er-
pington, Holt, and North } the town of Cromer — 1
Greenhoe — at

8th DISTRICT.

The hundreds of Difle, Earls-
ham, and Depwade, } the town of Diffe — 1
at

9th DISTRICT.

The hundreds of Gallow,
Smethdon, and Brother Crofs, } the town of Fakenham — 1
— — at

10th DISTRICT.

The hundreds of Loddon, Cla-
vering, and Henfted } the town of Loddon — 1
at

11th DISTRICT.

The hundreds of Tunfted, Hap-
ping, and South Erpington, } the town of North Walfham 1
— — at

🖎 Two are added to this number from the furplus.

NORTHAMPTONSHIRE.—Inhabitants, 158,000. M. P. 9, which are deficient to the number of people by 1. This county returns two reprefentatives on the landed intereft. It is divided into twenty hundreds, containing 326 . parifhes, and may be fubdivided into the fix following diftricts.

1ft DISTRICT.

Reprefentatives.

The hundreds of Nafaburgh, Willibrook, Polbrook, Corby, and Navisford — at } the city of Peterborough — 2

2d DISTRICT.

The hundreds of Spelho, New Bott Legrove, and Wimerfley ——— at } the county town, North-ampton. ——— } 2

3d DISTRICT.

The hundreds of Higham, Ferris, Huxlow, and Rothwell, ——— at } the town of Higham Ferrars 1

4th DISTRICT.

The hundreds of Faufley, Warden, and Norton, — at } the town of Daventry — 1

5th DISTRICT.

The hundreds of Towcefter, Clely, and Sutton — at } the town of Towcefter — 1

6th DISTRICT.

The hundreds of Hamford-fhew, Orlingbury, and Guilefburough ——— at } the town of Wellingborough 1

NORTHUMBERLAND.—Inhabitants, 142,000.—
M. P. 8, which are deficient to the number of
people by 1. This county returns two reprefentatives on the landed intereft; to which number,
being a large maritime county, may be added another, taken from the Cinque Ports. It is divided
into feven wards, containing 460 parifhes, and may
be fubdivided into the five following diftricts.

1ſt DISTRICT.

Reprefentatives.

The ward of Caſtle — at the county town, Newcaſtle *4

2d DISTRICT.

The wards of Iflandfhire, Glendale, and Bamburg, at } the town of Berwick —— 2

3d DISTRICT.

The ward of Coquetdale, — at the town of Alnwick —— 1

4th DISTRICT.

The ward of Morpeth, —— at the town of Morpeth — 1

5th DISTRICT.

The ward of Tindall —— at the town of Hexham — 1

* Two are added to this number from the furplus.

NOTTING-

NOTTINGHAMSHIRE.—Inhabitants, 168,000.—
M. P. S, which are proportionate to the number of
people. This county returns two representatives
on the landed interest. It is divided into six wapontakes, containing 168 parishes, and may be
subdivided into the five following districts.

1st District.

Representatives

The wapontakes of Thurgasson } the county town, Notting-} 2
and Ruscliff ———— at } ham ————

2d District.

The wapontakes of Newark } the town of Newark — *2
and Bingham, ———— at }

3d District.

The wapontake of Broxstow, at the town of Mansfield — 1

4th District.

The Hatfield division of Baf-} the town of Workfop ——— 1
, setlaw wapontake — at }

The North and South Clay di-}
vision of Baffetlaw wapon-} the town of East Retford — 1
take ————— at }

* One is added to this number from the surplus.

OXFORDSHIRE.

OXFORDSHIRE.——Inhabitants, 128,000.——
M. P. 9, which are proportionate to the number
of people. This county returns two reprefentatives on the landed intereft, and two reprefentatives are returned from the Univerfity of Oxford,
which return may ftill continue. It is divided into
14 hundreds, containing 280 parifhes, and may be
fubdivided into the five following diftricts.

1ft DISTRICT.

Representatives.

The hundred of Bullington and Wotton, — at } the city of Oxford —— *2

2d DISTRICT.

The hundred of Banbury, Bloxham, and Ploughley, at } the town of Banbury — 1

3d DISTRICT.

The hundreds of Binfield, Langtree, Ewelm, and Dor- chefter ——— at } the town of Henley —— 1

4th DISTRICT.

The hundreds of Tame, Lewk- nor, and Pirton, — at } the town of Tame —— 1

5th DISTRICT.

The hundreds of Bampton and Chadlington — at } the town of Witney —— 1

* One is added to this number from the furplus.

RUTLANDSHIRE.——Inhabitants, 20,000.—— M. P. 2, which are returned by the landed interest only. This county being so very small, one representative may be taken from the landed interest, and be assigned to the commercial, to be elected by delegates from every parish within the county, at the county town, Okeham.

SHROPSHIRE.—Inhabitants, 145,000.—M.P.12, which give a surplus of 3 above the ratio. This county returns two representatives on the landed interest. It is divided into 15 hundreds, containing 170 parishes, and may be subdivided into the seven following districts.

1st DISTRICT.

Representatives

The hundreds of Shrewsbury and Foord ——— at } the county town, Shrewsbury *2

2d DISTRICT.

The hundreds of Munslow and Overs, ——— at } the town of Ludlow ——— *2

3d DISTRICT.

The hundreds of Brimstry and Stottesdon ——— at } the town of Bridgenorth — 1

4th DISTRICT.

The hundreds of Parslow, Clun, and Chirbury, — at } the town of Bishop's castle 1

5th DISTRICT.

The hundreds of North and South Bradford ——— at } the town of Newport — 1

6th DISTRICT.

The hundreds of Wenlock and Cundover ——— at } the town of Wenlock — 1

7th DISTRICT.

The hundreds of Oswestry and Pimhill, ——— at } the town of Oswestry — 1

* One is added to each of these numbers from the surplus.

SOMERSETHIRE.——Inhabitants, 302,000.——
M. P. 18, which give a furplus of 1 above the
ratio. This county returns two reprefentatives on
the landed interest; to which number, being a
large maritime county, may be added another
taken from the Cinque Ports. It is divided into
43 hundreds, containing 385 parifhes, and may be
fubdivided into the nine following diftricts.

1ft District.

Reprefentatives

The hundreds of Hare Cliff, with Bedminfter, Portbury, and Chew —— at } the city of Briftol —— 4

2d District.

The hundreds of Bathforum, Keynfham, Wellow, and Chewton —— at } the city of Bath —— 2

3d District.

The hundreds of Wellsforum, Winterftoke, Bemftone, and Glafton Hydes — at } the city of Wells —— 2

4th District.

The hundreds of Taunton Dean, Andersfield, Kinfbury Weft, Melverton, North Currey, Abdick, and Bulfdon, —— at } the town of Taunton — 1

5th District.

The hundreds of North Petherton, Connington, Huntfpill, with Puriton and Whitley, —— —— at } the town of Bridgewater — 2

6th

6th DISTRICT.

The hundreds of Frome, Whitstone, Brewton, Norton, Ferrars, and Kilmerſdon, at } the town of Frome ——— 4

7th DISTRICT.

The hundreds of Caerhampton, Wilmington, and Freemannors, ——— at } the town of Minehead — 1

8th DISTRICT.

The hundreds of Tintinhull, Somerton, Martock, South Petherton, Kingſbury, and Crewkhorn ——— at } the town of Ilcheſter — 1

9th DISTRICT.

The hundreds of Horethorn, Cattesaſh, Stone and Yeovil, Berwick, Cocker, and Hunſbero, ——— at } the town of Milbornport — 1

* One is added to this number from the ſurplus.

STAFFORD.

STAFFORDSHIRE.—Inhabitants, 196,000.——
M. P. 10, which are deficient to the number of
people by 2. This county returns two reprefentatives on the landed intereft. It is divided into five
hundreds, containing 130 parifhes, each of which
hundreds may conftitute a diftrict.

1ft DISTRICT.

Reprefentatives
The hundred of Offlow, — at the city of Litchfield — 2

2d DISTRICT.

The hundred of Cudleftone, at the county town, Stafford 2

3d DISTRICT.

The hundred of Seifdon, — at the town of Wolverhampton 2

4th DISTRICT.

The hundred of Totmanflow, at the town of Uttoxeter— 2

5th DISTRICT.

The hundred of Pyrehill — at { the town of Newcaftle under line ——— } 2

SUFFOLK.

SUFFOLK.—Inhabitants, 202,000.—M. P. 16, which give a surplus of 4. This county returns two representatives on the landed interest; to which number, being a large maritime county, may be added another taken from the Cinque Ports. It is divided into 22 hundreds, containing 575 parishes, and may be subdivided into the nine following districts.

1st DISTRICT.

Representatives

The hundreds of Carlesford, Colneis, Sampford, and the Liberties of Ipswich, — at } the town of Ipswich — 2

2d DISTRICT.

The hundreds of Thingoe, Thedwastre, and Lackford, at } the town of St. Edmonds-bury ——— } *2

3d DISTRICT.

The hundreds of Baberge and Risbridge ——— at } the town of Sudbury — 1

4th DISTRICT.

The hundreds of Stowey and Blackbourn, ——— at } the town of Stowmarket — 1

5th DISTRICT.

The hundred of Loose, Wilford, and Thredling, — at } the town of Woodbridge 1

6th DISTRICT.

The hundreds of Hartesmere and Hoxon ——— at } the town of Eye ——— 1

7th DISTRICT.

The hundreds of Cosford, Bosmore, and Cleydon, — at } the town of Hadleigh — 1

8th DISTRICT.

The hundreds of Plumsgate, and Blithing ——— at } the town of Aldborough — 1

9th DISTRICT.

The hundreds of Wangford and Lothingland ——— at } the town of Beckles — 1

* One is added to this number from the surplus.

SURREY.—Inhabitants, 225,000.—M. P. 14;
which give a furplus of one above the ratio. This
county returns two reprefentatives on the landed
intereft. It is divided into 14 hundreds, containing
140 parifhes, and may be fubdivided into the fix
following diftricts.

1ft DISTRICT.

Reprefentatives

The hundred of Brixton, at the borough of Southwark *4

2d DISTRICT.

The hundreds of Woking,
Chertfey, and Farnham, at } the county town, Guildford 2

3d DISTRICT.

The hundreds of Kingfton and
Emly, ——— at } the town of Kingfton — 2

4th DISTRICT.

The hundred of Croydon and
Copthorne ——— at } the town of Croydon — 2

5th DISTRICT.

The hundreds of Ryegate, Dor-
king, and Tanridge, — at } the town of Ryegate — 2

6th DISTRICT.

The hundred of Godalming
and Blackheath — at } the town of Godalming — 1

* Two are added to this number from the furplus,

SUSSEX.

SUSSEX.——Inhabitants, 298,000.—M. P. 20, which give a furplus of 3 above the ratio. This county returns two reprefentatives on the landed intereft; to which number, being a large maritime county, may be added another, taken from the Cinque Ports. It is divided into 65 hundreds, containing 312 parifhes, and may be fubdivided into the 12 following diftricts.

1ft DISTRICT,

Reprefentatives

The hundreds of Bofeham, Weft Bourn and Singleton, Manhood, Aldweek, and Dumford ——— at } the city of Chichefter — 2

2d DISTRICT.

The hundreds of Barcomb, Dorfett, Loxfield, Rotherfield, and Loxfield Baker, at } the town of Lewis — 2

3d DISTRICT.

The hundred of Whaleftone, Prefton, Youfinere, Fifhers, Gater, Burbech, and Prefton, ——— at } the town of Brighton — 2

4th DISTRICT.

The hundreds of Guefling, Baldfloe, Bexhill, Nenfield, Battell, and Netherfield, at } the town of Haftings —— 1

5th DISTRICT.

The hundreds of Goldfpur, Staple, Goftrow, Henhurft, and Shoyfwell, — at } the town of Rye — 1

6th

6th District.

The hundreds of Grinftead,
Buttinghill,   Rufhmonden,   } the town of Eaft Grinftead   1
and Hartfield, —— at

7th District.

The hundreds of Eaft Eaftwrith,
Shinglecrofs, and Rother- } the town of Horfham —— 1
bridge —— at

8th District.

The hundreds of Eaft Bourne,
Longbridge, Dill, and Pe- } the town of Eaft Bourne — 1
fey Liberty and Foxearle,
—— —— at

9th District.

The hundreds of Avisford, Po- } the town of Arundel — 1
ling, and Brightford, — at

10th District.

The hundreds of Stenning,
Weft Grinftead, Windham, } the town of Stenning — 1
and Tipnoake, — at

11th District.

The hundreds of Eafbourne } the town of Midhurft — 1
and Weft Eaftwrith, — at

12th District.

The hundreds of Willingdon,
Alcifton, Totnore, Shiplake, } the town of Seaford — 1
and Hauxborough — at

WARWICK,

WARWICKSHIRE.—Inhabitants, 198,000.——
M. P. 6, which are deficient to the number of
people by 6. This county returns two reprefentatives on the landed intereft. It is divided into
five hundreds, containing 158 parifhes, and may
be fubdivided into the four following diftricts.

1ft District.

Reprefentatives

The hundreds of Knightlow, } the city of Coventry —— 3
and Coventry county at

2d District.

The hundreds of Kineton — at the town of Warwick — 2

3d District.

The hundred of Hemlingford, at the town of Birmingham 3

4th District.

The hundred of Barlichway, { at the town of Stratford on } 2
Avon ——

WESTMORE-

WESTMORELAND.—Inhabitants, 44,000.——
M. P. 4, which are proportionate to the number
of people. This county returns two reprefentatives
on the landed intereft. It is divided into four
wards, containing 26 parifhes, and may be fubdivided into the two following Diftricts.

1ft DISTRICT.

Reprefentatives
The eaft and weft wards — at the county town Appleby *2

2d DISTRICT.

The wards of Kendal and Lonf-
dale } the town of Kendal — 1
at

* One is added to this number from the furplus.

WILTSHIRE.—Inhabitants, 175,000.—M.P. 34, which give a surplus of 23 above the ratio. This county returns two representatives on the landed interest. It is divided into 29 hundreds, containing 304 parishes, and may be subdivided into the seven following districts.

1ft DISTRICT.

Representatives

The hundreds of Underditch, Downton, Cawden and Cadworth, Chalke, and Dauworth ———— at } the city of Salisbury —— 2

2d DISTRICT.

The hundreds of Swanborough, Melksham, Bradford, Whorwelsdon, ———— at } the town of Devizes —— 2

3d DISTRICT.

The hundreds of Selkley, Ramsbury, Kingsbridge, and Kinwaston, ———— at } the town of Marlborough *2

4th DISTRICT.

The hundreds of Malmesbury, Highworth, and Damerham, ———— ———— at } the town of Malmesbury — 1

5th DISTRICT.

The hundreds of Chippenham, Pottern Canigs, and Calne, ———— ———— at } the town of Chippenham 1 !

6th DISTRICT.

The hundreds of Amesbury, Elstube and Everley, Branch and Dole ———— at } the town of Amesbury — 1

7th DISTRICT.

The hundreds of Warminster, Westbury, Hatesbury, Damerham, and Mere, at } the town of Warminster — 1

*: One is added to this number from the Surplus.

WORCESTERSHIRE.—Inhabitants, 132,000.—
M. P. 9, which give a surplus of 1 above the ratio.
This county returns two representatives on the
landed interest. It is divided into five hundreds,
containing 152 parishes, and may be subdivided
into the three following districts.

1st DISTRICT.

Representatives

The hundreds of Worcester and Upton ——— at } the city of Worcester — 2

2d DISTRICT.

The hundreds of Blaken, Of-waldeslaw, and Pershore, at } the town of Evesham — 2

3d DISTRICT.

The hundreds of Halfshire and Doddigtree — at } the town of Kidderminster 2

YORKSHIRE

YORKSHIRE.—Inhabitants, 614,000.—M.P. 30. This extensive county returns two representatives on the landed interest; to which number may be added four more, taken from the Cinque Ports, which will give two representatives for each of the three ridings by which the county is divided. It is also divided into 24 wapontakes, containing 563 parishes, and may be subdivided into the nineteen following districts.

1st DISTRICT.

Representatives

The wapontakes of Bulmer, Ouse and Darwent, and Ansty Liberty, — at } the city of York — 4

2d DISTRICT.

The wapontake of Skirack, — at the town of Leeds — 2

3d DISTRICT.

The wapontakes of Harthill, Buckrase, and Hawdenshire, — at } the town of Beverley — 2

4th DISTRICT.

The wapontake of Morley, — at the town of Hallifax — 2

5th DISTRICT.

The wapontakes of Holderness, Dickering, and Kingston county — at } the town of Hull — 2

6th DISTRICT.

The wapontakes of Strafford and Tickhill — at } the town of Sheffield — 2

7th DISTRICT.

The wapontake of Agbridge, at the town of Wakefield — 2

8th District.

The wapontake of Barſton, — at the town of Pontefract — 2

9th District.

The wapontakes of Gilling Weſt and Hangweſt — at the town of Richmond — 2

10th District.

The wapontake of Hallikeld and Hang Eaſt —— at the town of Rippon —— 2

11th District.

The wapontake of Claro, — at the town of Knareſborough 1

12th District.

The wapontake of Staincroſs, at the town of Barnſley — 1

13th District.

The wapontake of Oſgodcroſs, at the town of Doncaſter — 1

14th District.

The wapontakes of Staincliff and New Croſs —— at the town of Settle —— 1

15th District.

The wapontake of Pickering, at the town of Scarborough 1

16th District.

The wapontake of Burdforth, at the town of Thirſk — 1

17th District.

The wapontake of Rydall — at the town of New Malton 1

18th District.

The wapontake of Lambargh the town of Guiſborough — 1

19th District.

The wapontake of Gilling eaſt and Allertonſhire — at the town of Northallerton 1

The

The Principality of Wales, confifting of twelve counties, fends to Parliament twenty-four Reprefentatives; twelve of whom are returned on the landed intereft, and twelve by the commercial; which as a province of the State, and of the leaft importance in the fcale of commerce, its products arifing chiefly from pafturage, may be confidered as equivalent to the number of inhabitants, which are computed at about 320,000. The only arrangement in this principality which may be propofed would be to elect the reprefentatives on the fame general mode of delegation as that offered for the Commons of England, and that two reprefentatives be returned from each county to join the Convention propofed for a Parliamentary reform.

Before a mode of reform be offered for a more equal reprefentation in Scotland, it may be ufeful to ftate the prefent mode by which the reprefentatives of the Scottifh Burghs are elected, which we learn by an addrefs from a committee of citizens at Edinburgh to the Burgeffes and Heritors *.
" Now we appeal to you, Gentlemen, how far
" you enjoy the invaluable privilege of election,
" which as Britifh fubjects is your birth-right.
" Do you elect your reprefentatives in Parliament?
" No—The Town Councils are the *fole* electors.
" Do you elect the Town Councils? No—The

* P. 13 and 14.

" Parliament

" Town Councils elect themfelves. Thus the
" Burgeffes of Scotland have not the moft diftant
" connexion with the legiflative body of the realm.
" They have not the moft *indirect* reprefentation
" to Parliament. The Councils are the abfolute
" electors both of themfelves and of our reprefen-
" tatives in Parliament. Can we then, Gentlemen,
" be faid to enjoy freedom or the rights of Bri-
" tifh fubjects ? Surely not. We leave it to your-
" felves, Gentlemen, to judge whether or not this
" be our prefent fituation. Are our reprefenta-
" tives in Parliament poffeffed of the qualities, or
" actuated by the principles of true patriots? Are
" they men of capacity and probity ? Are they ac-
" quainted with the ftate of our commerce and
" manufactures, and attentive to our intereft in
" Parliament ? No; intent only on procuring
" places and penfions for themfelves and adhe-
" rents, they will perhaps never think of the pub-
" lic welfare."

If this be the true ftate of the reprefentation of
Scotland, for the honour of their nation, refpect
for themfelves, and the fair fame of pofterity, the
people fhould never reft till they had obtained a
reform, otherwife thofe qualifications which tho
courtly intrigue of thefe laft thirty years has been
fixing on them by a few *bowing*, time-ferving,
cringing, infidious, mercenary, perfevering courtiers, will be confidered as hereditary.

However

However repugnant to conftitutional liberty the
prefent ftate of .the Scottifh Burghs may be, arbitrary in their police, and engroffed by an Ariftocracy, it has not a neceffary relation to the difcuffion which I have prefcribed myfelf. Their
internal police, however partially grievous, does
not affect the whole kingdom, for political liberty certainly does not depend upon the particular privileges or fetts of this or that Burgh, or any
particular cities or towns; on the contrary, they
depend on the free enjoyment of this principle
by the body of people. It is an univerfal power
fpreading over the whole State; it pervades the
clay-built hut as well as the ftately manfion; it
is a vital principle that fhould be cherifhed in
the bofom of the pooreft commoner, and by the
body of people fhould be ever maintained pure
for its own fake, and for ever be kept facred for
the bleffings of liberty, which it difpenfes to all.
That fo general a power fhould be prefcribed to a
local fituation, to one part of the State, and not to
the other, and confound the diftinction between
univerfal freedom and partial flavery, involves an
idea which equity and common fenfe revolts at,
and is wholly inimical to the principles of the
Britifh Conftitution. Upon the leading ones of
which, that there is no right without a remedy,
and that no individual can be bound but by laws
to which he fhall have given his confent through
the

the medium of his reprefentatives. There may be added therefore to the ten reprefentatives returned from each county in England two reprefentatives from each county in Scotland, compofing a convention fworn to the exprefs and only purpofe of eftablifhing an equal and adequate reprefentation of the Commons of Great Britain in Parliament. It may appear unneceffary to repeat, that a reform in Parliament can never be conftitutionally effected but upon the principles of political liberty before fully ftated. The fpirit of the laws of England would be deeply wounded, their texture violated, and the genius of the Conftitution utterly deftroyed, if in the prefent Parliament the idea of a fupreme and an arbitrary power were confounded. If it can disfranchife one borough, why not all? If it can enact its own exiftence from three to feven years, why not for a century, or decree itfelf perpetual. Political liberty is exprefsly againft fuch an ufurpation; no ftatute can deprive the people of thofe rights which are in themfelves unalienable. The right of chufing reprefentatives to legiflate, and the limitation of their exiftence in that capacity, is an undoubted right of the nation, it is the focial right of every man, which no pofitive law can wreft from him, which our anceftors could not difpofe of to the prejudice of their pofterity; and if any ufurped power fhould have violated this facred privilege, or if it fhould have been furrendered

dered by a corrupt Parliament, it can at any future time be lawfully refumed.

By the Act of Union, the number of reprefentatives from Scotland to the Britifh Houfe of Commons was fettled to be 45—thirty of which are returned on the landed intereft, and 15 on the commercial. The reafon for affigning double the number of reprefentatives to the landed intereft was of the fame impolicy which has influenced a number of Ariftocratic acts fince the Revolution. The queftion of importance between the landed and commercial intereft we can be at no lofs to decide, when we confider the growing affluence of Scotland wholly arifes from its manufactures and commerce; and from this fource alone depends the appreciation of land and the confequence of the landholders. As commerce therefore has become the firft moving principle in public affairs, and of the higheft importance to the State, the mode of reform which may be propofed for Scotland is the following.

That each fhire return one reprefentative on the commercial intereft, except the fmall fhires of Cromartie, Clackmannan, and Kinrofs; and that each reprefentative be elected at the principal town within the fhire, and be termed member of that town, but to be chofen by the delegates returned

by

by the ceſſed houſeholders of every pariſh within the county, as propoſed for England.

The delegates of the ſhire of Cromartie may be added to thoſe of Nairnſhire; the delegates of Clackmannan to thoſe of Sterlingſhire, and the delegates of Kinroſs to thoſe of Fifeſhire. By uniting theſe ſmall ſhires, there will remain an additional repreſentative to be elected at Edinburgh, Glaſgow, and Aberdeen; ſo that from theſe capital places may be returned 2 Members each to Parliament. This mode will give 33 repreſentatives on the commercial intereſt, and leave 12 for the landed intereſt, to be elected by the freeholders and copyholders, as propoſed for England; and theſe repreſentatives may be returned in the lowing manner.

The

The Delegates from the following Shires:

Edinburgh Haddington Berwick Roxborough Selkirk Peebles Dumfries Linlithgow Fife Clackmannan Kinrofs	} to elect at city of Edinburgh	4
Lanerk Wigton Air Kirkcudbright Bute Renfrew	} to elect at Glafgow	—— 2
Aberdeen Kincardine Bamff Elgin	} to elect at Aberdeen	—— 2
Perth Argyle Forfar Stirling Dumbarton	} to elect at Perth	—— 2
Invernefs Nairne Cromartie Caithnefs Sutherland Rofs Orkney	} to elect at Invernefs	— 2

——
12

That the delegates of the people should be put to no expence in their journies and waste of time to elect the representatives of the nation. Every shire in England, Wales, and Scotland, should, by a county rate, support the expence of elections, as well as the annual stipends which should be allowed to the national representatives during the continuance of a Parliament. On this last subject much has been said, and many are divided in opinion; but to me this observation appears unanswerable—The very texture of the Constitution is constructed on principles productive of a happy medium between the rigid principles of absolute Monarchy and the lax principles of Democracy. The same arguments therefore, taken in a constitutional point of view, will hold good against annual Parliaments as septennial; the first having a tendency to create anarchy, the other leading to arbitrary power; and as these arguments are clearly deducible from every constituent part of the Constitution, no doubt can arise that the industry and wisdom of our ancestors was even directed to the grand object of tempering the two extremes of absolute Monarchy and pure Democracy. The proper medium is therefore

TRIENNIAL PARLIAMENTS.

CON-

THE CONCLUSION.

AFTER contemplating the *Theory* of our Conªſtitution, and minutely ſurveying every part of a beautiful ſyſtem, erected by the wiſdom of ages, to counterpoiſe the inequality of men, to protect the virtuous from the vicious, the humble peaſant from the pampered Peer, we muſt unite in the ſentiments of eminent men of other nations, who adoring the Genius of Liberty which influenced the mind of Britannia, and adopted her the parent of Freedom, have confeſſed that ſhe has given to the world an emulative and grand ſyſtem of poliªtical economy; a ſyſtem which is gloriouſly inªtended to maintain the dignity of human nature, a ſyſtem, the genius of which it is to be hoped all nations may in time adopt.

But what muſt be the feelings, what muſt be the deep concern of the preſent age, to find this beautiful fabric has diverged by *practice* from that independence in its conſtituent parts which is its vital principle, and decayed in its ſtamina by a fundamental grievance in the repreſentation of the people ?

people ? The violation of the freedom of election, and the independence of Parliament, being universally acknowledged, should be with unanimity immediately remedied. Let not an enlightened people foster on posterity an evil, which increasing, may afford them no atonement but in the general execration of this, as a time-serving, corrupt, and degenerate age.

A partial reform of the rotten boroughs, and the neglect of a general organization of the elective power of the people, will be attended with the same effects. The first may give a colourable independence, but it will never produce that essential principle necessary to preserve the freedom of the Constitution, to maintain the independence of the people from the abuse of power, and to check that tide of luxury which is sapping the vitals of the State, and which will be the most formidable enemy the freedom of Britain ever had to encounter. Her arms deceive the eye, captivate the senses, indulge the passions, subdue reason, and triumph over reflection, enervate and weaken the powers of the Constitution, and sink a nation into vice and infamy. It was this which was both the cause of the splendor and decadency of the Roman Empire. It was this which rendered the Romans incapable of maintaining their liberties; and as every effect proceeds from a cause,

T   nations,

nations, like men, rife, flourifh, and decay; and doubtful would be the affertion, if a man fhall fay, we fhall avoid a fimilar fate.

The true fpirit of liberty is the real fpirit of the Conftitution; and every man whofe bofom glows with this noble flame, difdains the fpirit of faction; his heart exults in proud allegiance to that Supreme Power which guaranties his perfonal fecurity and private property. No greater wound can his feelings receive, than when ftern neceffity calls him forth to refift the abufe of a power created for his happinefs. His loyalty to his Sovereign, his attachment to the laws, and reverence for order, confpire to render him paffive and forbearing; and in the hope of a change of men, of meafures, and of time, he often fuffers anticipation of better days to fuperfede the energy of prefent vindication. But there is a time when even hope no longer can find a point to reft her foftering wing; thofe times have frequently occurred in the Hiftory of JOHN BULL; but the unity of his powers, and the energy of his fpirit, have ever regained the equilibrium; and he has taught the arbitrary Monarch, and the ambitious Ariftocrat, that their only fecurity and intereft is in the due exercife of their privileges, prefcribed by the laws; and that he himfelf, by knowing how to yield a grateful fubmiffion to a wife Go-

vernment,

vernment, has convinced all the world that he is capable of fecuring and enjoying the higheft poffible degree of human Liberty and focial Freedom.

F I N I S.

9 783337 077617